JUDICIAL ACTIVISM AND LOKPAL

JUDICIAL ACTIVISM AND LOKPAL

Edited by

Subhash C. Kashyap

UPPAL PUBLISHING HOUSE
NEW DELHI - 110 002 (INDIA)

UPPAL PUBLISHING HOUSE
3, Ansari Road, Darya Ganj, New Delhi - 110 002
Phones : *Off.* 3273756, 3286571, *Res.* 2242884

ISBN 81-85565-90-2
First published 1997

Printed in India

Published by B.S. Uppal for UPPAL PUBLISHING HOUSE 3, Ansari Road, Darya Ganj, New Delhi, Typeset by Telematics India, New Delhi and Printed by Arora Offset Press, 817, Guru Ram Dass Nagar, Delhi 110 092

'Remember' said John Adams, "remember democracy never lasts long. It soon wastes, exhausts and murders itself. There never was a democracy that did not commit suicide."

We must realise that this is entirely true, says Chief Justice M. Hidayatullah. Democracy must, to save itself, keep renewing itself. It is a form of government easy to establish, but difficult to maintain. As it represents a condition of society, we must strengthen our democratic institutions, by keeping them safe from corrupting influences. "Democracy" as McIver says "is not a way of governing whether by majority or otherwise, but primarily a way of determining who shall govern and broadly to what ends." It is a way of life and it must maintain human dignity, equality, and rule of law. It requires strong public opinion, independence and fearlessness in the press. It was said by Aristotle centuries ago, "the state is at its best when not the people but the laws govern and worst when persons with leisure make a profession of politics and govern others."

The institution of Lokpal is intended to keep politicians under check. We must first ensure that pseudo-politicians or politicians in disguise, do not enter the institution of Lokpal, otherwise, it will turnout to be one more institution like many other institutions about which we have all grown cynical. Lokpal should consist of not merely ex-judges, but statesmen of unimpeachable character. I am not so much worried about the method of their appointment. The question is who ultimately is appointed. Do they command the confidence of the nation is the real question.

An independent national council of twenty eminent men selected by the President himself, to advise on all matters on which the government is likely to take a decision in the interest of the political party to which it belongs is an experiment worth considering.

E.S. Venkataramiah
Former Chief Justice of India

PREFACE

It may sound strange but there is very close link between what has come to be known as judicial activism and the proposed Lokpal legislation before Parliament. In fact, the latest Lokpal Bill may have been conceived as the legislature's response to the way judiciary has been handling cases involving allegations of corruption among politicians.

The supreme credentials of legislators are that they are elected representatives of the people. They are sent to legislatures and paid from public funds only to serve the people and safeguard their rights and interests. They are not masters but servants. They cannot be above the law or a law unto themselves. The people have an inalienable right to monitor their conduct and to criticize, control and hold to account everyone of their representatives. In recent months, however, several attempts have been made to make politicians immune from public criticism and judicial scrutiny. Gist of three news items that appeared in the national press early this year is reproduced below:

(i) The Government has given a notice for the introduction of a Bill to amend the Constitution for "restoring the primacy of the executive in the appointment of judges." In effect, the powers now exercised by the judiciary in the matter of appointment of judges are to be taken over by the Government. Quite interestingly, it is said to be necessary to "ensure the independence of the judiciary."

(ii) There is enough evidence with the CBI in regard to a controversy hatched with the knowledge of the then Prime Minister Narasimha Rao to arrange payment of bribe to some MPs to purchase them to save his minority Government. But according to Rao, speaking through his counsel, ministers giving money to members of Parliament is not a bribe under the Prevention of Corruption Act. The acceptance of any gratification by the MPs or giving them money could not be construed as bribe. And, even if MPs were given bribe, it is not an offence under the Act.

(iii) Union Law Ministry is reported to have asked the Cabinet to approve moving of two bills to validate "notwithstanding any pending proceeding, judgement, order or decree of any court" all petrol pump/LPG and Kerosene dealerships and out-of-turn house allotment by Ministers. This will bail out relatives of politicians including the (then) Prime Minister's relative and help some 2000 bureaucrats.

Despite its misleading title, the Lokpal Bill also appeared to be directed to similar ends. With a view to creating awareness of the implications of the Bill and encouraging a wider public debate, *Politics India* co-sponsored a national seminar with the Citizenship Development Society, India International Centre, Institute of Public Administration and ten other organisations. A message received from the former Chief Justice of India Shri E.S. Venkataramiah is reproduced at the beginning of this book.

The present study brings together contributions by some of the most eminent jurists and scholars on the twin subjects. These contain valuable perspectives, perceptions and insights based on in-depth analysis of the themes.

The texts of the Lokpal Bill and the recommendations of the Parliamentary Standing Committee have been reproduced in Annexures for facility of reference. Several of the comments and suggestions made by the writers here seemed to have found favour also with the Parliamentary Committee and are reflected in their recommendations which, if accepted, would have the effect of improving the Bill considerably. Some fundamental objections would, however remain.

I am grateful to the eminent writers for their contributions and hope that the study would be read widely and with some interest and benefit. It may help the concerned citizens and readers to form their own views in the matter and to become active participants in the national debate.

Thanks are due to the publishers - Uppal Publishing House - for prompt and quality production.

New Delhi **Subhash C Kashyap**
15 August 1997

CONTENTS

CONTRIBUTORS

1. Justice ***H.R. Khanna*** is the distinguished former Judge of the Supreme Court and an eminent jurist.

2. Justice ***P B Sawant*** is the President of the Press Council of India and a former Judge of the Supreme Court.

3. Professor ***P.V. Indiresan*** is Visiting Professor at the Centre for Policy Research, former Director I.I.T. Madras, Professor at I.I.T. Delhi and President Indian National Academy of Engineering.

4. Dr.***G.R.S. Rao*** is Director Centre for Public Policy and Social Development, Hyderabad.

5. Dr. ***Sunder Raman*** teaches Political Science at the University of Delhi.

6. Shri ***S.D. Bali*** is a Political analyst and activist.

7. Shri ***Nafees Ahmad*** is a researcher in Law, Aligarh Muslim University.

8. Shri ***Niranjan Sahoo*** is a researcher in Political Science, University of Hyderabad.

9. Dr. ***Subhash C Kashyap*** is Hon. Visiting Professor at the Centre for Policy Research, Hon. Editor *Politics India* (Monthly) and Nehru Fellow for 1996-98. He was Secretary-General Lok Sabha during 1983-1990.

10. Shri ***U C Agarwal***, IAS (Retd) is former Central Vigilance

Commissioner.

11. Dr. ***Bindeshwar Pathak*** is founder Sulabh International Social Service Organisation.

12. Shri ***J. Veera Raghavan***, I A A S (Retd) is Director Bhartiya Vidya Bhawan and former Secretary Ministry of HRD, Government of India.

13. Dr.***S.S. Singh*** is Professor of Justice and Administration, Indian Institute of Public Administration, New Delhi.

14. Dr.***R.D. Sharma*** is Professor of Political Science and Dean Social Sciences, Himachal Pradesh University, Shimla.

15. Dr***Abdulrahim P. Vijapur*** is Head Centre for Federal Studies, Hamdard University, New Delhi.

16. Dr.***Surat Singh*** is Advocate Supreme Court of India.

17. Dr.***Suresh Kulkarni*** is an Associate with the Institute of Peace Research and Action.

18. Dr.***Mohinder Singh***, IAS (Retd) is former Secretary, Ministry of Shipping and Transport, Government of India

PART ONE
JUDICIAL ACTIVISM

1

JUDICIAL ACTIVISM

Courts As Trustees of the Constitution

H.R. Khanna

While discussing the topical subject of Judicial Activism, it is necessary to remove and clear certain mental cobwebs. A number of people look upon judicial review of the laws made by legislature and acts of the executive as a piece of judicial activism. It is a wholly misconceived notion. Our Constitution enshrines a number of fundamental rights guaranteed to the people. It further contains an express provision in article 13 that any law inconsistent with or in derogation of the fundamental rights shall be void to the extent of such inconsistency. The article also provides that the state shall not make any law which takes away or abridges the fundamental rights and any law made in contravention of this clause shall, to the extent of contravention, be void. The word 'law' mentioned in the article includes any ordinance, order, byelaw, rule, regulation and notification. It is provided that the right to move the Supreme Court for enforcement of the fundamental rights is guaranteed. The Supreme Court has, for the purpose, been vested with the power to issue directions, orders or writs in the nature of Habeas Corpus, Mandamus, Prohibition, Quo Warranto and Certiorari, whichever may be appropriate for the enforcement of the fundamental rights. Likewise, power has been conferred on every high court to issue for the territories in relation to which it exercises jurisdiction to any person or authority, including any government within those territories, directions, orders or writs in the nature of Habeas Corpus, Mandamus,

Prohibition, Quo Warranto and Certiorari, for enforcement of the fundamental rights and for any other purpose.

It follows from the above that it is the Supreme Court and the high courts which have been vested with the power to afford redress to the aggrieved party in case there is violation of fundamental rights and for any other purpose. The courts, in doing so, do not act as super-legislatures but only in the discharge of obligation that has been imposed upon them by the express provisions of the Constitution. The US Constitution did not contain any express provision for judicial review and the power was carved out by the US Supreme Court under the stewardship of Chief Justice Marshal in the case of *Marbury vs. Madison* which evolved the principle of judicial review. As against that, our Constitution contains express provisions to that effect. It is also noteworthy that in exercising the power of judicial review, the courts cannot and do not go into the wisdom behind the laws made by the legislature. Their function primarily is to look into the constitutional validity of those laws and decide accordingly. Apart from the laws made by the legislature, the courts also look into the validity of the acts of the executive in order to ensure that they do not infringe the provisions of the Constitution and are also not violative of the statutory laws made by the legislature.

The investigating agencies and the vigilance cells, till about a year or two ago, shirked from their duty in investigating gross acts of political corruption and amassment of ill-gotten wealth by ministers and other high personages because the investigating officers were subordinate to and under their administrative control. As such, they were turning a blind eye to such acts of political corruption and amassing of wealth lest they offend their bosses. The judiciary, has removed the shadow of fear and made the investigating officers to enforce the rule of law so that none may carry the notion that he is above the law.

View has been expressed and complaint has been made by many in the political field that the judiciary, in making the investigating agencies to look into the acts of political corruption and amassment of ill-gotten wealth by political bosses, has over-stepped the limits of its authority. This too is an erroneous idea. It is one of the primary functions of the judiciary to ensure the rule of law. The investigating agencies and the vigilance cells, till about a year or two ago, shirked from their duty in investigating gross acts of political corruption and amassment of ill-gotten wealth by ministers and other high personages because the investigating officers were subordinate to and under their administrative control. As such, they were turning a blind eye to such acts of political corruption and amassing of wealth lest they offend their bosses. The judiciary, in doing so, has removed the shadow of fear and made the investigating officers to enforce the rule of law so that none may carry the notion that he is above the law. The judiciary has upheld the basic principle that howsoever high one may politically or administratively be, the law is above him and he cannot avoid the penalties for the infraction of the law. It is as a result of ensuring the rule of law that many skeletons in the cupboard of ministers and other political highups have been revealed and acts of amassment of huge amounts of wealth through corrupt means have come to light. As such, any charge against the judiciary of having over-stepped the limits of its authority by enforcing the rule of law, is wholly ill-founded.

At the same time, it needs to be emphasised that it is the elected representatives of the people enjoying the confidence of the legislature and answerable and accountable to the people at the time of elections who have to govern the country with the help of civil servants. Care has, therefore, to be taken to ensure that the courts do not usurp the functions of the executive agencies. There have been occasions, the critics point out, that in issuing directions in matters which are administrative and about which the courts do not possess the requisite expertise and proficiency, they have over-stepped the limits. Such decisions, it is stated, land the administrative agencies in practical difficulties and make them bear the brunt of judicial decisions, some of which were wholly oblivious of the administrative needs, and, as such, ill-conceived.

There have also been occasions when the courts have issued directions to local bodies and other agencies as to how they should run their administration. Criticism against such decisions is levelled on the ground that once the courts take it upon themselves the task of issuing ukases as to how local bodies and other agencies should run their administration, what is there, consistently with the above approach, to prevent the courts from issuing directions as to how the State governments and the central government should administer the States and the country. Would not such an approach disturb the delicate balance of distribution of powers and functions between the three wings of the state - the Legislature, the Executive and the Judiciary? Would not such approach strike at the very basis of our democratic polity which postulates that the governance of the country should be carried on by elected representatives of the people enjoying the confidence of the legislature and answerable and accountable to the people at the time of elections? Would it not result in judicial oligarchy dethroning democratic supremacy? The governance of the country, it is pointed out, is the most complex task demanding a high degree of statecraft. It calls for decisions many of which and the reasons behind many of which cannot, without jeopardising the security of the country and the well-being of the people, be divulged or discussed in open. The governance of of a country or a State is a task assigned by the Constitution to the respective governments. These governments are headed by the Prime Minister or the Chief Minister, as the case may be, and his Council of Ministers and they in their turn are responsible to the duly elected legislature. It is no function of the courts, the critics assert, to attempt to assume such awesome responsibility even on a limited scale. The courts, according to them, should never assume and never be tempted to assume such domineering role. The country can ill-afford to be governed through court decrees. Any such attempt will not only be grossly undemocratic, it would be most hazardous and may result in national disaster. In this context, critics reiterate that the court, ordained as a judicial body, cannot be looked to as a general haven for reform movements.

> ***The trouble arises when one wing of the state tries to encroach upon the field of the other. It is in the above context that special responsibility devolves upon the judges to avoid the over-activist role and to ensure that they do not over-step or trespass upon the sphere earmarked for the other wings of the state.***
>
> ***The courts, have to be much more circumspect in ensuring that they do not overstep the limits of their powers, because to them is assigned the function of being the guardian of the Constitution. It is a faith and trust reposed by the framers of the Constitution in the courts and their position in this respect is akin to that of a trustee.***

Our Constitution has demarcated different fields of operation of the three wings of the state. As long as each organ of the state operates within its demarcated field and shows due deference for the other two organs, no difficulty would arise in the working of the Constitution. The trouble arises when one wing of the state tries to encroach upon the field of the other. It is in the above context that special responsibility devolves upon the judges to avoid the over-activist role and to ensure that they do not over-step or trespass upon the sphere earmarked for the other wings of the state. In certain situations the appeal has to be to the legislature or the executive and the judges ought not to be seduced by quixotic temptation to encroach upon other fields to set right every fancied wrong paraded before them.

The bosom of the judiciary, it is asserted, is not wide enough for all kinds of hopes and fears of men nor is it in a position to provide solution for any and every problem, although human ingenuity would not be lacking to give it some kind of shape or semblance of a legal or constitutional issue. A judge like Epictetus, it has been aptly put, must recognise the impropriety of being emotionally affected by what is not under one's control. The courts, it is also pointed out, have to be much more circumspect in ensuring that they do not overstep the limits of their powers, because to them is assigned the function of being the guardian of the Constitution. It is a faith and trust reposed by the framers of the Constitution in the courts and their position in this respect is akin to that of a trustee. When the other agencies or wings of the state overstep their limits, the aggrieved parties can always approach the courts and seek redress against such transgression. When, however, the courts themselves are guilty of such transgression, to which forum would the aggrieved parties appeal? If mankind, while passing through the successive stages of political consciousness, has done away with despotism of kings and dictators, it would be puerile to expect it to put up with despotism of judicial wing of the state. Of the different types of depotism, judicial despotism is not only inexcusable, it is also most irrational.

2

JUDICIAL ACTIVISM

Trends and Prospects

P.B. Sawant

'Judicial activism' has been debated and discussed for the last some months in the media and on the public platform, because of the popular interest evinced in some orders passed and decisions given - mostly the former, by courts right from the Apex Court to the magisterial court of the land. These judicial pronouncements related, either to the acts or omissions of individuals holding, or who had held high offices in public life, or to matters of interest to some sections of the society, or to the nation as a whole. The popular interest aroused by these pronouncements was only to be expected, but the discussion on their merits and demerits has not always been well-informed.

Nature and Parameters of Judicial Function

The function of the judiciary in any society is to adjudicate disputes which come before it. The disputes may be between individuals, or between private individuals and institutions on the one hand and the public institutions and authorities including government on the other, between two State governments or between the State government and the central government. The dispute may also be between the society or a section of the society and some private individuals and private or public institution or government. The disputes have to be resolved by interpreting and applying law to them. The law includes not only the fundamental statute, *i.e.* the Constitution, and the other statutory law but also the legal precedents *i.e.* the judge made law, the jurisprudential principles and the inherent powers vested in the courts by the statute to do complete justice in a matter. The courts express their views on matters which come before them. They do not and cannot hunt for matters, nor can they choose them. They are under an obligation to decide all matters coming before them, and they cannot refuse to decide them, except on grounds of personal involvement in the matter. The hearings in the court are public, and the courts are required to give written reasons in support of their decisions. The decisions are public documents. The courts are bound by the law, and the legal precedents while deciding matters. They have to deal with all arguments advanced before them by both sides, and give legal reasons, for accepting or rejecting them. The decisions of the lower courts are liable to be scrutinised by the higher courts. Even the decisions of the Supreme Court are liable to be reviewed by the same Benches or the larger Benches. The decisions may also be scrutinised, debated and discussed by the public, and the students of law on the public, fora and in the media, and the flaws therein may be pointed out publicly. The scope for free play of the personal views of the judges, however meritorious the views may be, is therefore limited. There is thus an in-built accountability of the judiciary.

Imperatives of Judicial Function

Whatever the skill of the draftsman, many times there remain in the legislation weaknesses in the form of faulty language, ambiguities, inconsistencies and even contradictions, expressions which are capable of meanings more than one, incongruous phraseologies and so on. It is the function of the courts, to give a harmonious interpretation to the legislation, consistent with its intention, and to save it from being reduced to an absurdity or an unworkable law. This exercise may, on occasions require the court, to supply words and expressions, modify the language, impose inarticulate presumptions, and even do a bit of redrafting of the legislation, to bring it in conformity with the original intention of the legislature. This is an essential part of the judicial function, and has to be undertaken, to further the intention of the legislation and to save it from being rendered otiose.

It is implicit in the judicial function of interpreting and applying the law to the facts of the individual case, that the court treats the law as an ever active and a live instrument, and applies it to all situations which it is intended to cover.

Further, no legislation can take into account all present and future situations and their permutations and combinations. Life is complex and ever changing, and the human nature and conduct are unamenable to stereotypes. The law is and has to be based on certain common presumptions which may not hold good on all occasions. No society can make law to meet every situation. The judges, as authorities entrusted with the task of applying the law, are expected to extend the law to all situations, normal or abnormal, contemplated or not contemplated at the time of making the law, to enforce the solemn intention behind the law. By doing so, the courts prevent the defeat of the objective of the law and uphold its majesty. Human ingenuity is unlimited and can always pick loopholes to circumvent the law. The courts, while discharging their function, therefore, owe a duty to the society to defeat the machinations of the law-breakers, and to uphold the rule of law. So long as the courts make the extensions of law to cases, which are intended to be covered by its spirit, though not always by its letter, which can at no time be all comprehensive, the courts discharge their essential duty of enforcing the law. Such extension and application of law is a functional obligation. This applies also to the application of the judge-made law or the legal precedents.

The courts have been indulging in these exercises for all times since the beginning, in furtherance of their duty to do justice and to uphold the rule of law. These exercises have been variously called the "judicial legislation", "interstitial legislation", "plugging the loopholes", "filling the gap" etc. They are not only not resented but welcome, and lauded as a necessary part of the judicial work. In the absence of such initiatives taken by the courts, the law will remain ineffectual most of the time and inoperative in respect of most of the situations, requiring the legislature to amend it limitlessly. The attempt by the courts on such occasions to apply the law being founded on, and within the framework of the law, is unexceptionable. It is a therapeutical input flowing organically from the law itself.

Judge-made Law

Besides the "gap-filling" and the "extension" operations, the courts have to undertake a different kind of exercise, when they are faced with disputes where the issues involved are not either wholly or partly covered by the statutory law. The courts in such cases resort either to the existing jurisprudential principles or evolve new principles or use their inherent powers to do justice between the parties. The equity law is wholly evolved out of this benign process.

The common law of England is an outstanding example of the judge-made law and has stood the test of time. The courts do not and cannot remain silent in the absence of the statutory law. True to their office, they have to resolve the disputes coming before them and ordinarily cannot refuse to entertain them or throw their hands up on the specious plea of the absence of the law. The judges are called upon, in such circumstances, to bring to bear upon the issues, their learning, their training, their wisdom and perspicacity and to evolve just, proper and durable guidelines to resolve such and similar issues. In this process they are undoubtedly guided by the existing norms and values and practical considerations. The jurisprudence of every legal system is the product of such evolutionary process, which in turn aids and assists the development of law, including the statute law. The just, equitable and normative principles are as much necessary for administering the law as for making it. The evolution of such principles and of the law based on them is conducive to the growth of a healthy legal and judicial system and is a built-in part of it. It is not judicial activism but a necessary part of judicial mechanism.

Constitutional and Statutory Objectives and Provisions

Constitution of any country is its fundamental law and its objective and provisions are binding on all individuals and institutions in the society. It is the duty of all to further its objectives and abide by its provisions. All laws and orders, notifications and rules, policies and programmes, decisions and adjudications, norms, values and principles must conform to the Constitution and promote its goals. More so, it is the duty of the three pillars of the State, to enforce it in spirit and letter. Although it is self-evident, and not necessary to emphasize, article 51A (a) of our Constitution makes it a duty of every citizen to abide by the Constitution and to respect its ideals and institutions. While adjudicating matters before it, the judiciary is therefore required to keep in mind all the provisions of the Constitution and to give effect to them so far as it lies within the purview of its judicial functions of resolving disputes. Its decisions have therefore to be in conformity with the provisions of the Constitution and it has to strike down acts which go counter to them. When the judiciary discharges this role, keeping in mind that the separation of powers is as much an inseparable part of the Constitution as the power of the judicial review, it acts as ordained by the Constitution. It does not thereby become activist. It discharges its mandatory constitutional function of keeping the individuals and institutions within their constitutional bounds and directing them to perform their affirmative constitutional obligations.

What is true of the role of the courts, with regard to the constitutional goals and provisions, is also true with regard to the statutory objectives, injunctions and obligations. It is the function of the courts to enforce them. In none of the above operations *viz,* while filling the gaps, making organic extension of the law, evolving judicial tools for doing justice or enforcing the mandatory provisions of the Constitution and the statutes and furthering their goals, can it be said that the judiciary is indulging in exercises which are beyond its proper sphere of activity.

Concept of Judicial Activism

It will not be wise to attempt a positive definition of judicial activism, much less a comprehensive one. The occasions on which activism may be attempted and the manner and the extent to which it may be indulged, may vary according to the exigency, the opportunity and the need as also the inclination, the perception and the philosophy of the judge. Broadly speaking, judicial activism falls into two categories. One is largely acceptable while the other is not permissible at all. The first consists of evolving new principles, new concepts, new maxims, new formulae, new equities, new procedures and new reliefs going beyond and sometimes even alien to the hitherto known and evolved jurisprudence and subtantive and procedural law. The second extends to laying down priorities, policies and programmes and giving directions to execute them when they are not obligatory, and are entirely in the discretion of the executive and the legislature or other authorities, and thereby usurping their function, power and wisdom; to taking over detailed administration of a policy, scheme or programme even if they are obligatory instead of monitoring their performance; giving directions to execute a plan or a policy in a particular manner when equally good or better alternatives are available; preventing implementation of schemes and projects on grounds unsupported by and unverified with the expert knowledge; interfering with the working of the independent autonomous bodies by meddling with their decisions for no reason other than their alleged impropriety; foisting the court's choices, directing enactment of laws when they are at best directory; interpreting Constitution and statutes contrary to their language and original intention, or by going beyond their accepted and well established and understood meaning, so on and so forth. In short, exceeding the constitutional brief of interpreting and applying the law as it is, and taking over executive and legislative functions in violation of the constitutional scheme of the separation of powers.

Organic Innovations and Extensions

The judges, particularly of the higher courts like the Supreme Court and the High Courts, are not expected to be automatons. Doing justice is not a mechanical process. Each case differs from the other. The stereotyped justice is contrary to the concept of justice itself, for justicing implies and involves every time, a fresh application of mind, interaction with the parties and their lawyers, appreciation of the oral and documentary evidence against the particular background of each dispute, of the arguments advanced and the relief sought. The judges are required to be live partners in the process of justicing and to respond creatively to the demands of justice in each case.

Creativity and innovation are as much necessary in justicing as impartiality and independence. The judges are not expected to be mere mechanics and masons. They are required to be designers and architects. So long as their innovations are within the bounds of their jurisdiction and are designed to advance the cause of justice, and do not do violence to the legal norms, however unorthodox and unprecedented they may be the innovations have to be welcome as accreditions to the legal armoury to preserve and promote justice which should be the object of any legal and judicial system. It is true that the certainty of law is a hallmark of the rule of law and the majority of the judges stick to the trodden path. But that is no reason to frown upon innovations which are designed to promote and strengthen the rule of law. Creativity is not given to every individual. But it is creativity which has marked the progress of mankind in every sphere. The growth and development of law over the years owes itself to the bold initiative and innovations of the few who thought positively and constructively and refused to submit helplessly to the impasse, or to the dead-end situations created not necessarily by the law but by its development till that stage. That category of the acts of judicial activism which evolve new principles, concepts, maxims, formulae and reliefs to do adequate justice, or to expand the standing of the litigant and open doors of the courts for the needy, or to entertain litigation affecting the entire society or a section of it as in the case of public interest or social action litigation, has not only to be welcome but encouraged. The critics of such judicial activism stand on a less sure ground when they assail it for no other reason than that, it introduces innovations and disturbs the existing calculations and certainties of the law. The certainty of law is not a virtue, beyond a certain limit, and when it is desired at the cost of justice, it is not a cherishable value. Justice should be the first consideration of all legal and judicial systems. Law is created by man to serve him and to do justice. He may modify it for the same purpose.

> ***The certainty of law is not a virtue, beyond a certain limit, and when it is desired at the cost of justice, it is not a cherishable value. Justice should be the first consideration of all legal and judicial systems. Law is created by man to serve him and to do justice. He may modify it for the same purpose.***

That is why the criticism of the public interest or social action litigation or epistolary jurisdiction when it was innovated, could not be appreciated. Fortunately, it has since become a part of our legal weaponry and has been assimilated as a judicial procedure. Were it not for that, the naked violation of the basic human rights as witnessed in the *Bandhua Mukti Morcha case, Bhagalpur Jail Blinding case*, and in the crop of cases which followed them, complaining about the trampling of human rights in jails, police custody, mental asylums, women's rescue homes and childrens' remand homes would not have come to light and the victims would not have received the relief in terms of damages, compensation and rehabilitation. What is of further importance is the awareness it created among all concerned that those incarcerated in such places are as much under the protection of law as others and that the persons in charge of them are equally accountable to the society. Before that, it was not the rule of law but the rule of thumb, of those in charge, which prevailed, a situation which was certainly not creditable to any free society. It can hardly be contended that the courts should have waited to remedy the situation till the legislature had made suitable changes in the law, procedural or substantial. Taking cognizance of the cases requiring justice and doing justice to the needy is properly the function of the court and in innovating the new procedure the courts acted in furtherance of their duty. It would have been a travesty of justice if the court had thrown its hands up in desperation for want of the requisite procedure. The procedure is a hand-maid of justice and not *vice versa*.

Criticism of Judicial Activism

The criticism of judicial activism is not uniform. Some welcome the first kind of activism, while deprecate the second. The same persons who criticise one on some occasions, welcome it on other occasions. As one western jurist has put it: "it all depends on 'whose ox is gored'." It is many times the interests and not the principles which dominate either the glorification or condemnation of judicial activism.

Some critics denounce all changes in the *status quo* on various grounds. It will be convenient to deal with their criticism briefly here.

In compelling the authorities to do their mandatory duties under the law, or to refrain from doing them against law, or in setting aside the accomplished illegal acts, the judiciary only performs its duty.

It is said that judiciary encroaches upon the jurisdiction of the executive, the legislature and other independent and autonomous institutions in its activist role. In the first instance, the majority of the cases, where the courts have directed the authorities to perform certain things or to refrain from others, the acts have been such as the authorities were duty-bound under the law to perform or to refrain from performing. In compelling the authorities to do their mandatory duties under the law, or to refrain from doing them against law, or in setting aside the accomplished illegal acts, the judiciary only performs its duty. There are exceptional cases where the judiciary can be said to have usurped the powers of the executive or the legislature or other authorities. It is these few cases which are played up and an impression is created that the judicary generally strays into the areas of the other institutions.

There have no doubt been few instances where the judiciary has out-stepped its brief. When the Parliament was directed to enact Common Civil Code, when percentage of seats for all India students was fixed for medical course in all universities, when fees were fixed for students of medical course all over the country, when examinations held and the admissions to courses and recruitment to services were cancelled on non-substantial grounds, when electoral programmes were set aside for unavailable and impermissible reasons, when direction was sought to be given to include a player in a cricket team and so on, the court did exceed its jurisdiction. Fortunately, such cases have been few and far between.

The second objection to judicial activism is that the judiciary enters an area where it has no expertise and competence to undertake the regulation and management of the affairs. The history of the cases so far shows that the courts have entered such arena only when compelled to do so for reasons of law and have taken precaution to be guided by experts in the field. Many times some things are allowed to perpetuate in some of the institutions and establishments in the name of confidentiality, safety, security etc. Even a little probe sometimes reveals that the matters are deliberately kept mysterious for the benefit of the vested interests. The courts by and large have refrained from disturbing the framework and the functioning of such establishments and given direction only to remove patent illegalities and injustice.

It is also contended that courts are indulging in activism at the expense of their normal adjudicatory work, and this is one of the reasons responsible for the huge arrears of cases. This criticism has no basis in fact. The statistics show that the public interest litigation or the cases where the court assumes the allegedly "activist role", constitutes a negligible proportion of the total number of cases. It is not that every judge is seized of the "activist cases" or the judges are occupied with such matters all the time. Such cases, by their very nature, attract attention of the people and the media and are alone reported. An impression is therefore created that the courts do not do other work. There is no evidence to show that the cases where the judiciary had assumed "activist role" have affected the disposal of the other cases in any significant way. And assuming it has, whose interests should weigh more, of the society at large or a large section of it or of the individual litigants ?

The last but not the least important criticism is that the judiciary may lose the confidence of the people if its directions given in such cases are not complied with. As pointed out earlier, the judiciary most of the time gives direction to perform the mandatory duties under the law. It leaves the implementation of the direction to the authorities themselves and only monitors compliance by calling for reports. Secondly, the judiciary has the power to punish for the non-compliance of its directions by invoking its contempt powers. The experience shows that the authorities do heed the court directions.

The criticism against judicial activism forgets that in democracy no elective authority willingly undertakes measures, however beneficial they may be in the interests of the nation, if such measures are likely to cost it votes of some or the other section which is likely to be affected by the measures. It is then left to the judiciary which has no vote bank to look to, to compel the authority to perform its obligatory duty for the benefit of the society. In fact, many times the executive, the legislature and others on their own throw the ball in the court of the courts and desire direction from them to undertake the measures which they also believe to be in the best interests of the society. It is further not correct to say that the people are likely to lose confidence in the courts because of their "activist" role. The people have instead started looking to the court as their only saviours with the executive and the legislature taking an indifferent stance towards their problems.

> ***The criticism against judicial activism forgets that in democracy no elective authority willingly undertakes measures, however beneficial they may be in the interests of the nation, if such measures are likely to cost it votes of some or the other section which is likely to be affected by the measures. It is then left to the judiciary which has no vote bank to look to, to compel the authority to perform its obligatory duty for the benefit of the society. In fact, many times the executive, the legislature and others on their own throw the ball in the court of the courts and desire direction from them to undertake the measures which they also believe to be in the best interests of the society.***

Usurpatory But Largely Ignored Activism

The very critics ignore that the greatest innovation was made by the Supreme Court in no less a law than the Constitution when in the face of the unambiguous language of article 368 which permits Parliament to amend any part of the Constitution, the court spelt out the theory of the basic structure of the Constitution prohibiting the Parliament from amending certain parts of the Constitution. So is the innovation introduced by the Supreme Court in the matter of appointment of the High Court and Supreme Court judges, by appropriating the powers of the President to itself, inspite of the clear language of the relevant provisions of the Constitution. Of the same piece are the decisions of the U.S. Supreme Court in *Dred Scott case*, the commercial clause and the *New Deal legislation cases* and *the desegregation cases*. Which of them represented judicial activism?

Was the court playing an activist role when it declared that the Negroes (Blacks) were not the citizens of America and that the labour welfare legislation was against the Constitution or when later it upheld the right of its black population to the citizenship, the labour welfare legislation as constitutional and segregation as opposed to the equality clause of the Constitution? The instances can be multiplied but it is not necessary to do so here. What is of importance for our purpose is to note that judicial activism is only selectively criticized and the criticism is not always value based.

> ***While it is incumbent upon the courts to enforce law and the mandatory duties under it rigorously, it is equally expected of them to recognise and respect their own constitutional limits. This is particularly necessary when under our Constitution the judiciary has the last word. The excesses of judiciary may disturb the balance between the three institutions and trigger off a constitutional crisis.***

Dangers of Judicial Activism

Nothing is an unmixed blessing. Although what the people have commonly come to dub as judicial activism is no activism. There is a danger, that carried by its momentum, the judiciary may extend it to areas which do not properly belong to it as has happened in the few instances in the past. It is therefoe necessary to sound a note of warning while even making allowance for the fact that to err is human and judges after all are also human. The Constitution envisages separation of powers among the three institutions of the State and each is expected to keep itself within its limits. Self restraint is as much necessary as a responsive approach. Give unto others what is theirs. While it is incumbent upon the courts to enforce law and the mandatory duties under it rigorously, it is equally expected of them to recognise and respect their own constitutional limits. This is particularly necessary when under our Constitution the judiciary has the last word. The excesses of judiciary may disturb the balance between the three institutions and trigger off a constitutional crisis. The court must also guard against entertaining litigation at the instance of the rival interests. There are instances where beneficial measures, schemes and projects are sought to be scuttled for political and economic considerations and the public interest litigation is instigated and even financed by the interested hostile individuals and organisations. If the courts do not circumspectly scrutinise each litigation which comes before it in the name of public interest, the danger is that the judicial activism in some cases may prove a curse instead of a boon to the society.

The danger seems more pronounced today with the wide publicity given by the media to the judicial pronouncements. That is likely to encourage populism and a race for one up-manship among the judges. The judges are neither saints nor superior beings. They are subject to the same human weaknesses and failings. In their enthusiasm to do something novel they may overdo their part. Populism is worse than corruption. While corruption affects parties to a litigation, populism affects the entire society by the wrong precedents. What is worse, it affects independence, fairness, objectivity and impartiality and consequently the confidence of the people in the judiciary which is its only asset. If the judiciary thus gets destroyed, that will be the end of the rule of law. The media should therefore desist from publicising the names of the judges while reporting their orders and judgments. It is sufficient to say that the court whether the Supreme Court, High Court, the District Court or the magistrate, passed the order. The people are not interested in knowing the names of the judges.

The forays of the judiciary in the fields of the other institutions which fortunately are few and peripheral today, if become intrusive, may also invite a backlash from the other institutions and at times even from the affected people, particularly, when they touch the socio-economic, religious and cultural issues. This has happened in the past. Such reaction may make the judiciary over-cautious and reticent in discharging even its legitimate duties. That will be a negative development. The important thing therefore is to always bear in mind the limits and not to transgress them. The judges may venture organic innovations in law to develop it but should not adventure their personal predilections and philosophies, and substitute their wisdom, and their notions of justice and propriety of good and bad, for that of the executive and the legislature. Much less should they appear arbitrary and high handed however righteous their reaction.

Peep in the Future

The future course of the judicial activism *i.e.,* the initiative the courts are taking to enforce the rule of law by requiring the mandatory duties to be performed and by preventing and setting aside illegal activities, and by granting relief to the deserved, will depend upon several factors. The composition of the courts, the perception and the inclination of the judges, the awareness of the people, the alertness of the social action groups, the response of the executive and the legislature and the other public institutions to the needs and grievances of the people, the delays, indifference, waste, inefficiency and corruption on the part of the implementing machinery, the extent of the arbitrary exercise of power and of the denial and trampling of human rights, the denial of civic facilities, the destruction and pollution of ecology and environment, and *et al.*

It is wrong to look upon the judiciary either as a saviour or as a trigger-happy institution. The judiciary cannot solve all problems since it can play only a limited role of ensuring accountability to the rule of law where the law is either transgressed or not complied with. At the same time, the judiciary will be too happy to be left alone to do its normal work of adjudication of disputes between the parties. It is circumstances which compel it to intervene and assert its role as the guardian of the law when the law is not respected by those who ought to enforce it.

It is wrong to look upon the judiciary either as a saviour or as a trigger-happy institution. The judiciary cannot solve all problems since it can play only a limited role of ensuring accountability to the rule of law where the law is either transgressed or not complied with. At the same time, the judiciary will be too happy to be left alone to do its normal work of adjudication of disputes between the parties. It is circumstances which compel it to intervene and assert its role as the guardian of the law when the law is not respected by those who ought to enforce it. The judicial activism so called will recede in proportion to the recession of the disregard of the law. The reaction of some members of the executive and the legislature to the judicial activism is not well considered. The attempt to exclude some public offices from the Anti-corruption Act and the restrictions reportedly sought to be placed on public interest litigation, if true are steps which to say the least are ill-advised. While the former measure is debatable, the latter will clearly interfere with the powers of the court and particularly the constitutional powers of the High Court and the Supreme Court to regulate its own procedure.

> ***The government, by appointing ex-judges to the political offices of Governors, has exposed itself to the legitimate criticism of attempting to hold carrots before the judiciary and to erode its independence. That such a step should have been taken by a government which is a coalition of thirteen different parties and is supported by one of the major parties is a development of grave concern to the nation.***

While these measures are obviously intended to restrict the jurisdiction of the courts, the government, by appointing ex-judges to the political offices of Governors, has exposed itself to the legitimate criticism of attempting to hold carrots before the judiciary and to erode its independence. That such a step should have been taken by a government which is a coalition of thirteen different parties and is supported by one of the major parties is a development of grave concern to the nation. Nothing short of an unanimous resolve by the Parliament that such an exercise will not be repeated in future, will quieten the just fears of the society in that behalf. One only hopes that in the meanwhile the judges on their part will not allow themselves to be swayed by such sops. But if it happens that may be the end not only of the judiciary's activist role in ensuring the rule of law but of its independence itself.

3

REFORMING INDIAN JURISPRUDENCE

An Engineer's View

P.V. Indiresan

It is said that it is slippery at the top. The reputation of Indian judiciary is at its peak, or close to it. The last time, Indian judiciary commanded such high respect was in the early years of independence when the Supreme Court pronounced several far reaching judgements. Pandit Nehru, himself a lawyer, took umbrage and clipped the wings of the Supreme Court in no uncertain manner. Later his daughter Indira executed a virtual *coup de grace.* History may not repeat itself, modern day politicians may not have the power and the prestige that Nehru commanded, or the wilfulness his daughter had. Yet, judges would be unwise to forget that it is indeed slippery at the top. So, this is not the time for euphoria but for caution. It is also important to remember that the sudden upsurge in the respect the courts command has come about mainly because there has been a marked improvement in the disposal of cases that concerns common people. Courts remain a forbidding, intimidating, awe-inspiring edifice. No doubt that is how it ought to be. At the same time, the courts should inspire confidence that they are the protectors of the last resort. There is much doubt whether our courts do indeed inspire such confidence.

Our legal system is largely inspired by Roman jurisprudence. Frankly, many in the legal profession are opposed to our own tradition of justice, and even ashamed of it. No doubt *Manu Smriti* is archaic, and untenable. Even so, any legal system we practice should match our culture, any alien imposition is unlikely to be very effective. For instance, consider the veracity of witnesses. In the Christian tradition, it is considered unthinkable that a person would lie after swearing on the Bible. Though the *Upanishads* exhort *satyam vada,* the devout Hindu has no compunction to lie to protect his family, his kin or his *jaati.* For a typical Hindu, the court is not a moral place but a bargaining market, or a battle arena where his knight in armour engages in combat with that of his opponent. That kind of attitude spills over to other communities also with the result that truth is murdered systematically in our courts. Yet, we do have places where truth is sacrosanct. A notable case is that of *Dharmasthala* in Western Karnataka where no Hindu dare tell a lie before, of all persons, a Jain priest! So, our people are not against truth, the courts do not offer the ambience that will inspire them to stick to the truth in general, the Indian litigant goes to court not to secure justice but to settle scores. Sadly, many legal practitioners encourage such an attitude. The judicial system we have borrowed from the British must have some basic mismatch with our culture for our courts to bring out the worst in our people who are otherwise not as bad as they behave inside courts. Everyone in the legal profession should ponder why that is so.

History may not repeat itself, modern day politicians may not have the power and the prestige that Nehru commanded, or the wilfulness his daughter had. Yet, judges would be unwise to forget that it is indeed slippery at the top. So, this is not the time for euphoria but for caution. It is also important to remember that the sudden upsurge in the respect the courts command has come about mainly because there has been a marked improvement in the disposal of cases that concerns common people. Courts remain a forbidding, intimidating, awe-inspiring edifice.

Courts constitute the arm of the government that enforces justice. How that may be done is described very elegantly in the *Bhagavad Gita* which explains that the establishment of *dharma* involves two tasks: one, *paritraanaaya saadhoonaam,* two, *vinaashaayacha dushkrutaam.* British jurisprudence takes an extreme view of the first task of protecting the innocent by enjoining on the courts that it is better that a hundred guilty escape rather than one innocent person be wrongly convicted. The result is, our courts perform poorly when it comes to the second task of destroying evil doers. That is why crime has escalated as much as it has in the past few decades. We blame politicans for promoting crime. The courts should also bear their share of the blame for protecting criminals as much as they have done. As honest frustrated police officers will vouch, the courts in India have all sympathy for the criminals, and none at all for the victims of crime.

Communication engineering teaches us that every decision is subject to two kinds of errors. Translating to the judicial system, they are, one, punishing the innocent, and two, exonerating the guilty. Both types of errors are unavoidable however wise the judges may be. The best that may be attempted is to minimise—not the errors - but the consequences of the errors. Then, we should enquire whether current practices of jurisprudence are optimum in the sense that they are the best for society at large. For instance, there are many serious cases of corruption, and outright criminality that are being investigated by the courts. The common view is, the criminals will escape, and will continue to lord over the polity unchecked. According to the strict laws of evidence, that is not an improbable scenario.

As Abraham Lincoln complained, Roman jurisprudence is over sensitive to property rights, and quite insensitive to human rights. Mahatma Gandhi was closer to fair play when he held property to be not so much a right as a trust. Consider the case of a legislator charged with a serious offence. He can browbeat the administration not to bring forward any charge. Even if that is done, he can induce concerned officials to make a faulty charge so that he gets discharged. He may be convicted (though so far that has been a virtual impossibility). Even then he is free to appeal until kingdom come. All the while he can employ corruption and intimidation to get elected and re-elected. He can also become a minister and even have a say in the appointment of judges. All this is permitted on the ground that he has a constitutional right to be a legislator until it is proved beyond doubt that he is guilty of a serious crime. That right he can exercise by intimidating (even eliminating) witnesses. He then goes Scotfree, enjoys the privileges of power and wealth and remains immune to any threat from the law.

On the other hand, there are the weak who have no protection from the law. We know of several scientists who have been charged with treason, kept in prison for years and finally discharged because no evidence was produced. They lost their jobs, their reputation and in law they have no hope of getting any compensation. Ordinary people are harassed by corrupt officials all over the country. Because of current rules of evidence, and because the jobs they hold is treated as a property right, they do not get punished-particularly if they are powerful. It is a peculiar situation the state (read for the state, corrupt officials and politicians) can harass any honest citizen with impunity, and the aggrieved citizen may not secure the protection of law for years, if ever. At the same time, these powerful people go Scotfree by the same law. There lies the weakness of Indian jurisprudence, and a threat to its sanctity.

There are two fundamental issues here. One is insufficient protection afforded to the general public from the depredations of powerful criminal elements. The other is delay. Though it is said, "justice delayed is justice denied", a former Supreme Court justice has said "justice hurried is justice buried!". Particularly in property matters, Roman jurisprudence makes a mockery of justice even in crimnal cases.

There is a need to consider not merely protection of those charged with crime but also social consquences of such protection. Then, it is worth making a distinction between a privilege and a right. To vote in elections is a right, but to stand for elections is a privilege. A murderer cannot be allowed to mock the public, stand for elections on the ground that there are no witnesses to prove him guilty, and there are no witnesses because they too have been killed.

At the present time, proof of guilt beyond doubt is demanded. That is one extreme end of the full range of proof. By confining itself to this extreme corner, the entire judicial process is getting unbalanced. There is a need to consider the other end of proof also: 'proof of inocence beyond doubt'. Then only in cases where rights are involved, proof of guilt beyond doubt may be insisted, but as a counterbalance, wherever privilege is involved, (anything which provides control over society is a privilege), the burden of proof should change from one of guilt beyond doubt to one of innocence beyond doubt. Then, for instance, anyone who aspires to be a legislator has to prove beyond doubt that he or she is innocent of criminal behaviour. It is possible that a truly innocent person may not be able to furnish such a proof, and hence be denied a chance to contest. Yet, it is safer for the society at large that a hundred innocent persons be denied the privilege to contest elections rather than one criminal be let loose in the legislative arena. That is a fair balance to the judicial view that it is better that a hundred guilty go unpunished rather than one innocent person be penalised. Preventing a person from occupying a position of privilege might be a personal (even a social) loss, but that is no punishment. After all, as Gray's Elegy puts it: Some mute inglorious Milton here may rest, some Cromwell guiltless of his country's blood.

So, getting into positions of privilege is a matter of rare chance. Nature denies that chance to many deserving people. That being the case, there is no point in offering pointed judicial protection to the undeserving, no point in letting Gresham's Law take over, and help the bad drive away the good.

As the common saying goes: what matters whether *Rama* rules or *Ravana* does! So, most people are not concerned about people in power (though, for the judiciary that ought to be a matter of nominal concern). For ordinary people, property disputes are of greater anxiety. It is a peculiar feature of Western jurisprudence that there is almost never a dispute about who owns a car or any such movable property, but when it comes to immovable property, the disputes are endless, and it takes years to get a final judicial verdict, if ever. It may not be far wrong to say that the entire legal profession treats the time of the client with contemptuous indifference. There is something fundamentally wrong with the whole process. It is time to think of something better.

One such possibility emanates from digital systems which have to make millions of decisions every second. In a digital system, the concern is not where the truth is. Instead, the question that is decided each time is which side is closer to truth? The verdict is given entirely in favour of the side which is closer to truth and entirely against the side that is farther from truth. At present, the fashion in civil disputes is one of arbitration, of deciding the fine line of exact truth does not exist at all. Then, we are engaged in a futile exercise in 'searching in a dark room for a black cat' which is not there. Not surprisingly, civil cases take years to conclude and even then satisfy no one.

If, instead, we apply the digital technique, the judge will have no responsibility of deciding the exact truth between the two conflicting positions, but only to choose the one or the other. At the present time, in the hope of pulling the judgement in their way, litigants make extraordinary demands. If Rs. 100,000 is a reasonable compensation, one party may demand a million while the other may offer only a 10,000. Even if the judge decides correctly for the figure of 100,000, neither party is satisfied. One side dreams of getting a million shattered, and the other is infuriated at what it considers to be an extortion. So, appeals are made, and the dispute never ends. In a digital system, the judge is free to award either a million or 10,000, and nothing in between. That forces each side to be ultra-cautious, not to stray too far from a reasonable value. One side may then demand Rs. 120,000 while the other may offer 85,000. Observing that the opponent is closer to the realistic value, and fearing a major loss, the first one may scale down the demand to 105,000. In any case, the probability is the two parties will pitch in very close to each other—in stark contrast to the present system, where they stake their claims poles apart. Because there is a compulsion to be reasonable, the dispute may not reach the courts at all, and even if it does, the verdict will give comparatively little heartburn. The verdict also can be reached fast because one need not be bothered by minute nuances, and only the broad picture has to be scanned. It is no accident that digital systems are mind bogglingly fast—and versatile too.

Our judges periodically express concern at judicial delays, and about ever increasing backlog of cases. They are symptoms, not the disease itself. So, the problem will not be solved by increasing the number of judges. Parkinson's Law applies here too: the number of cases (and appeals) will increase as the number of judges increase. So, what we need in this connection is not quantitative increase but a qualitative reform, a new paradigm. In any field of knowledge, a change in paradigm occurs only when new ideas are grafted on to the old, and not by tinkering with the existing system. The green revolution solved our food problem, and saved our country from starvation, not by using more of the old seeds but by introducing new hybrid ones. As Thomas Kuhn has forcefully agrued it is that lesson which intellectuals tend to avoid because they are comfortable with the old. At times, some one breaks the mould, and makes bold to explore outside the trodden domain for new ideas. Then, and only that way, can we expect a new paradigm, and make qualitative progress. At this moment, our judicial system does need a new paradigm. Let us hope we will get one soon. Let us pray that will be well before criminal elements hold our country to ransom.

4

POLITICAL POPULISM, ADMINISTRATIVE CAREERISM AND JUDICIAL ACTIVISM

Distortions in the Process of Democratic Social Transformation

G.R.S. Rao

There are five parallel tracks on which the process of social change is taking place today. The five tracks are not mutually exclusive, but are activated concurrently by different groups of people. The nature of density of these five tracks is shifting with the changing dispositions towards, and patterns of use of these tracks, reflecting the quality of democracy and degrees of anarchy in India. These five tracks are depicted in the form of an illustration followed by a summarisation of the ever increasing shift from the democratic to the anarchic mode of social change.

Constitutional-Democratic Mode

In a constitutional democracy, such as India, the constitutional scheme provides the direction, the pace, and the mechanism for bringing about social transformation; the legislative, the executive and the judicial instrumentalities of state perform different and yet complementary tasks in order to achieve their inseparably common objectives. Representative, decentralised political process, and a responsive and responsible executive with accountability for results and transparency in performance operating as the 'first-court-of-justice', almost makes the role of judicial institutions redundant excepting where validity, interpretation and application of law or the Constitution are involved as a part of the process of dispute settlement and conflict resolution. Dedication to the constitutional values, goals and processes on the part of the functionaries manning these three institutions would promote social harmony and (harmonious) development, as the two wheels of social transformation. In the background of this ideal canvas, what is the Indian reality?

Ideal and the Reality of the Political/Legislative Process

Under ideal conditions, the democratic process is nourished and sustained by the political/legislative process, harmonising the diversity and conflict of values and interests. Mahatma Gandhi had stated that the "lives of millions of people constitute my politics." Politics thus equated with service to the society inspires the manifesto of political parties, influences the mandate of the people, shapes the programmes, the well-being of all the citizens, and quality of life of the community as a whole - enhancing the sense of citizenship through processes such as decentralisation and participation.

In reality today, the wide-range of distortions in the political/legislative process can be summarised thus : (a) a shift in the motive-force of political process from 'public-service' to 'personal-power', acquisition of power at any cost, and retained at all costs (as reflected by increasing degrees of money and muscle power, muscle-power getting into the legislatures, converting people into vote-banks, and competitive populism) leading to the disastrous consequence of fracturing the society; expanding patterns and intensity of corruption (covering recruitment, postings, transfers and promotions, to gas and telephone connections, to railway berths); devaluation of the intrinsic value of votes' (starting with Rs.5/- paid as a price for the vote of a citizen during the 1950s to the elimination of voters and the candidates in the election process, and, as of now, purchase of votes within the legislatures, and corrupting even the system of parliamentary and legislative committees. In sum, politics have defected from the people; political parties have become the single largest `corporate' activity geared to the amassment of power and pelf : `power' has become the prime-mover of politics with no place for social development, and nation-building. The potential threat of corruption to democracy in India emerges from the fact that almost

51.0 per cent of the citizens have become collaborators in corruption, thus debasing the democratic base.

> ***Politics have defected from the people; political parties have become the single largest 'corporate' activity geared to the amassment of power and pelf: 'power' has become the prime-mover of politics with no place for social development, and nation-building. The potential threat of corruption to democracy in India emerges from the fact that almost 51.0 per cent of the citizens have become collaborators in corruption, thus debasing the democratic base.***

Indian parliament did not, repeat not, have to bring about the 73rd and 74th amendments to the Constitution in order to set in motion the process of decentralised, participative, self-reliant, sustainable development. The process of amendments with all the political breast-beating was a redundant exercise. And, having brought in the amendments, they have been already aborted, nay snuffed out, *a la infanticide* through authoritarian political process and even worse, centralised bureaucracy. Anti-defection legislation was an equally redundant measure; no true democracy ever had to invent such a measure; having brought it into existence, it is being abused in a manner precisely contrary to its proclaimed objectives.

Indian legislatures, including the national, are churning half-backed legislation; occasionally with the privately admitted hope, that such legislation would be questioned in and quashed by the judiciary. The avalanche of legislation is not backed up by the intention and ability to implement, inspite of the knowledge that such legislation can only backfire. Social transformation is mocked through churning of political declarations. Indian political process today has become anarchic at all levels. The impression that sections of politicians project today is that even crimes such as a gang-rape or a dacoity can be got condoned or even legitimised by manipulating numbers in the legislatures, as if numbers are all about democracy.

Ideal and reality of the administrative process : When the gravity of the political process is firmly rooted in the society, it is adequately, if not absolutely, supported by the administrative structures, systems and processes in translating political will, into delivery of efficient and effective service, thus promoting justice political, economic and social. Under ideal conditions, administrative process is characterised by commitment to the Constitution and to the policies of the party in power as mandated by the people, responsive to the problems and needs of the people; responsible to the elected representatives; transparency in performance and democratic in style. Under ideal conditions, administration can truly operate as the change-agent, the instrument of social transformation and as the 'first-court-of-justice'. 'feedback' is provided to the political executive and to the legislatures on the inadequacies and unintended distortions in the policies and programmes so that appropriate mid-course corrections are provided by the political/legislative processes. People's 'problems', 'grievances', or 'complaints' at the individual as well as the systemic levels are received and processed as the built-in 'management information system' in providing correctives to the administration, and thus preventing recurrence. Such an ideal disposition on the part of administration would eliminate the need for citizens to seek either 'politicisation' of their problems, or to secure the intervention of the judiciary.

An alert administration committed to the constitutional mandate could check the abuse of power at the political level, monitor and control the factors that cause social turbulence and violence leading to breakdown of law and order, and thus uphold the rule of law - the quintessence of democratic social transformation. Thus, under ideal conditions, administration should aim at zero complaints and grievances against the state.

In reality, the democratic constitutional republic is distorted and aborted by the executive as well through centralisation, authoritarianism and non-responsive disposition, sans accountability and transparency. In spite of the 73rd and 74th amendments to the Constitution, adopted on the basis the experience and wisdom of seven five year plans that development cannot be effectuated without democratic decentralis ation, development effort continues to be been effectively neutralised by the centralised bureaucratic structures,systems and styles. The political executive, irrespective of party affiliations, has consistently charged, *ad nauseam*, that bureaucracy in India has become the major impediment to social transformation.

Administration has not merely remained an impediment or barrier to social change, it has also effectively negated all attempts at reforms. The Republic is left with several prime ministers and chief ministers lamenting the fact, as if they were helpıess. The citizens are left with the committees and commissions that only resulted in escalated charge on the public exchequer, and volumes of wisdom converted into garbage by the efflux of time, belying and burying the hopes of reform. The only change that the administrative apparatus of the state has been affected, with deadly periodicity, is through a series of pay commissions. The administration in India has grown into a mighty self-serving corrupt citadel of power.

Indian political process today has become anarchic at all levels. The impression that sections of politicians project today is that even crimes such as a gang-rape or a dacoity can be got condoned or even legitimised by manipulating numbers in the legislatures, as if numbers are all about democracy.

The 'average citizen', including women and children, works for 350 days in India; the government servant pushes the files for not more than 150 days; government servants take more than 85 paise out of every rupee revenue of the state, the community gets something out of the balance of 15 paise. Alas, in the Indian republic today, they are not accessible to the 'average citizens'; they look down upon the citizens as lesser mortals.

All the ombudsmen institutions ranging from anti-corruption bureaus; grievance and complaint mechanisms; vigilance cells and commissioners; Lok Ayuktas and the much debated Lokpal; and a wide range of other national and State level commissions (women, human rights, minorities, *et al*) and institutions have not been able to mitigate, much less eradicate the problems of citizens with the administration. Even worse, there has emerged a pattern of equations between the political and administrative functionaries in the form of collusion, the latest scenario reflected in the Vohra Committee Report, as 'nexus', politicians and the administrators have entered into collaborative exploitation with extended participation by the criminals. There is a visible and measurable slide in the umpiring of Indian democracy, belying the efforts and hopes of the founding fathers of the republic.

The 'average citizens' disposition towards the political/legislative as well as the administrative institutions and processes is characterised by alienation antagonism and hostility leading towards fatalistic withdrawal on the one hand, or an inclination towards partnership in corruption with the politicians and the administrators, or even worse, taking law into their own hands on the other, with disastrous consequences to the polity. The fourth category, increasingly becoming a declining minority, go to the judicial institutions in the hope of either providing a corrective, and/or securing justice. This category is tending to become not only a declining minority, but also 'cynical', for the other categories of citizens mock at them as the 'unwise', and offer to 'tout' their cause - a process of negative 'conversion'.

The Judicial Process

When the political/legislative process is lost in competitive populism, and in the exclusive pursuit of power at an enormous social cost and as the administrative process has become self-serving, the dammed social problems explore alternative tracks, in search of solution. That is how, in India today, the judicial process seems to have moved to the centre-stage.

Under conditions of a democratic decentralised polity, the ideal of '*Rama Rajya*' should have been 'empty-court-rooms, and 'zero-litigation' - between citizens as well as between citizens and the State.

In reality, we are not only carrying on with an antiquated legal system and judicial process without even an alibi available after 50 years of independence for its continuance with its adversarial, litigation-prone, time-consuming, hierarchical layers of the system. The system frustrates the law-abiding citizens most; the conscientious members of the judiciary are equally frustrated with the realisation that they are manning a system that has become dysfunctional and counter-productive. All this inspite of accumulated knowledge, experience and wisdom borne out by the volumes of reports being churned out by the national and State level law commissions, and various other commissions and committees that invariably end up, *inter-alia,* with a beaten path of recommendations *viz,* (a) amendments to the existing provisions of law (b) improvement in the content and quality of legal education and (c) increasing the number of judges at various levels. An adjunct to this set is the reform in the judicial structures, process, training and continuing education for members of judiciary at all levels. India has excelled all other countries (developed and developing), and itself, in creating ever new institutions, an institutional proliferation, but certainly not in creating a 'work-ethic'.

That the statistics of pending cases of litigation presented to the Parliament and to the State legislatures, periodically and in a routine manner, are not only staggering, but are also grossly misleading is known to everyone. Everyone of the lawmakers, law-enforcing functionaries, justice administrators, law-breakers, and the hapless citizens is aware that for every one 'problem' that contributes to the statistics of pending cases, there is atleast one, if not two, that has/have not entered into the official statistics. Knowledgeable and wise citizens recognise that taking their problems to the judicial institutions will lead to more frustration, more expense, aggravation of conflict, and that the court system, if ever, can be expected to deliver justice to the second generation of litigants.

There is not merely a tremendous amount of filtration (complaints are not registered, often the aggrieved party is slighted, insulted and even abused in a variety of ways beyond the verbal, in police stations) but also distortions galore at the chambers of advocates, and in the court premises; it is corruption all around not merely monetary, but corruption in all its Indian manifestations. It has become proverbial, and continues to be, that it is the rich, 'influential' and knowledgeable who threaten the poor, the weak, the innocent and the ignorant, that they will be 'dragged to the court'. That is why in the reality of life, people opt out of the system, making the statistics of pending cases most unreliable and misleading. The innocent, who have no other means of pursuing redressal of their problems, are aware that it is the rich, the influential (haven't we got anticipatory bails for criminals) and the underworld who are abusing, and are allowed by the system to abuse the judicial process. There was a judge who while dealing with alienation of tribal land, rather unwittingly stated "but what would happen to the 'poor' people who invested a lot of money on the lands?"

Even more dangerous to the republic is the image, that is gaining ground, of systemic inadequacies and distortions in the appointments, transfers and elevations of members of the judiciary, and increasing degrees and myriad forms of corruption creeping into the system.

True to the extant culture of governance in India, transfer as an effective instrument of 'punishment' is being used even in the case of judiciary. Even worse, post retirement appointments have emerged as 'rewards' alongside the liberalisation of the Indian economy. Providing legislative cover to such appointments represents another form of degeneration, and loss of credibility of the judicial system.

Vibrancy of Democratic Base and Declining Standards of Institutions of State: True to the inherent attributes of democracy, which is otherwise vibrant at its base, the alert citizens aided by the more 'concerned' functionaries manning the legislative, administrative and the judicial institutions, are activating the two complementary institutions *viz.*, citizens' initiatives (variously called non-governmental organisations, community-based organisations, etc.) and earlier the print and now also the electronic media, constituting the vital fourth and fifth estates respectively of democracy. While peoples' initiatives are taking several paths, they find the judicial institutions more responsive, contributing to the emergence of public interest litigation as the third track of social transformation.

The vibrancy of democracy in India is reflected, *inter-alia*, on three occasions in the short span of five decades; first, when the dictatorial tendencies in the form of 'emergency' had been nipped in the bud by the people; second, when the legislation seeking to censor the media had to be withdrawn; and third, efforts to curb public interest litigation were made futile by strong public opinion. That there are distortions even in the functioning of the media and the community-based organisations cannot constitute a case against their role and place in democracy.

Public Interest Litigation

Public interest litigation (PIL) cannot be legislated, for if and when an attempt is made to do so, it ceases to be PIL, but becomes a part and parcel of the formal legal system and of judicial process. It can retain its creative character only when it is operated outside the formal legal system. And, as long as it is not statutorily defined, opinions are bound to vary about the concept and its role and place, including its tenability and desirability. Even if and when it is defined and regulated, the citizens of the republic should be given the credit for the gift of innovative exploration of alternatives, options and choice; and equally, members of the judiciary are bound to explore and innovate creatively, as has been the case during the four decades, though conditioned by individual dispositions and varying styles in their effort to respond to the dynamics of the society. Article 32 of the Constitution provides a safety-valve in the best interest of the constitutional republic.

Under ideal conditions, PIL should operate as a safety-valve, as the third track of social transformation, under, and in tune with the spirit of the Constitution. It speaks of the good sense of the government of the day that the (ill-conceived) proposal to regulate and restrict the scope of public interest litigation has been dropped.

But, an inherent danger to the PIL becoming counter-productive could emanate from the judicial institutions themselves rooted in the citizens' experience with the clogged, dilatory, non-responsive character, and image distortions of the judicial process, systems and styles. While public interest litigation has to be allowed to operate in an atmosphere of judicial innovation, the ebb and tide of PIL is already being attributed to the populist dispositions of individual members of higher judiciary. It is also acquiring the colour of judicial surfing into the realm of policy, that belongs to the political process.

Thus, unless and until the clogged channels of the judicial system are quickly cleared and made adequate, and the philisophical premises and judicial dispositions are crystallized with a large measure of sharing, the third track also may get distorted as indeed there are indications, going by the labelling of public interest litigation variously as judicial activism, populism, extremism, absolutism and adventurism.

> ***Knowledgeable and wise citizens recognise that taking their problems to the judicial institutions will lead to more frustration, more expense, aggravation of conflict, and that the court system, if ever, can be expected to deliver justice to the second generation of litigants.***

Quality of Democracy and Degrees of Anarchy : The three tracks *viz.*, (i) political/legislative and administrative, (ii) the judicial institutions and processes, and that of (iii) public interest litigation are perfectly within the realm of democratic constitutional mode of social transformation. However, the pattern of their activation at any given point of time reflects the quality of democracy.

Inter-institutional and intra-institutional tensions, contributing to their relative efficacy, provide for the germination of alternative paths of social change, leading to varying degrees of anarchy. Democracy as well as anarchy can coexist to some extent, and for some time. In India today, the process of governance and social transformation are showing clear signs of rapid slide from the democratic mode to the anarchic path. There are two discernible tracks - (a) the extra-legal-institutions and processes and (b) the various shades and streams of extremist organisation and processes that are tending to bypass the legitimate modes in constituting the fourth and fifth tracks leading the republic in the direction of anarchy. Any bypass would, sooner than later, lead to,making the original dysfunctional, leaving the substitute as the only path of social transformation in political process, (blood circulation in physiological terms). It is not only that the quality of democracy is showing signs of degeneration, but the degree of anarchy is rising fast and the system of governance as well as the polity are heating up.

Extra-Legal Institutions and Processes

An 'average' Indian citizen today does not respect a police constable as the symbol of the majesty of law; citizens fear the police and would like to avoid any contact, or a visit to a police-station for a variety of reasons; yet, the police is approached if circumstances so compel not knowing where else to go. The image of police is that they operate as an extralegal force; the constabulary believe and opine that they are not protected by their own leaders if they act under conditions of strict legality. It is not only the police, but the entire range of institutions designed to sustain law and promote justice.

The founding fathers of the Constitution had the vision to provide for constitutional machinery with immense design safeguards in forms such as Tribes Advisory Councils, comprising the elected representatives of the tribal communities in order to protect the interests and to promote the welfare of tribal communities. But, the impact of five decades of their 'existence' can be summed up in that they have not only failed to fulfill their constitutional role, but in fact proved counterproductive in more ways than one. The cancer of corruption is illustrated in cases such as prohibition/excise officials themselves indulging in the trade of illicit liquor, and the vigilance and anti-corruption officials conniving with and protecting the corrupt.

The extra legal institutions and process can be seen as emerging from disuse, abuse and misuse of the statutory and constitutional processes by all the instrumentalities of the state.

Abuse of legal institutions can at best be illustrated in terms of partisan dispositions and other inadequacies leading to the emergence and growth of private armies; ' modernisation' of the police forces to the utter neglect of the compelling need for professionalisation; and abuse of the police leading to their awareness of the declining image and efficacy with the disastrous consequence of demoralisation, giving rent to their frustrations in the form of brutal violence against unarmed innocent citizens. The paradox of public policy and police in India is that in five decades the State governments have been dismissed or administration has been taken over more than a hundred times, on grounds of break-down of law and order; all political parties in-office had been accused by all parties in opposition of misusing and abusing the police force (in a variety of ways); yet, no political party has brought in the 'State Security Commission' as a buffer between the political process and the police, designed to protect both, and to help enhance impartiality and accountability of police. Strangely, the leadership of police organisations has also not so far made it an important issue, thus giving the impression that they are comfortable with their own political equations, even if resulting in disastrous consequences to the rule of law, loss of morale of the police forces, and increasing incidents of state terrorism. In the case of judicial institutions, the image has gained ground that distortions are creeping into the system through instances such as "bail" being abused, and is being allowed to be so abused, especially by the affluent. The ever shifting policy and practices in regard to appointment, transfer, elevation and appointment to commissions; the mix-up between privileges and prerogatives; have not enhanced the image of the judiciary among the citizens. Judicial activism may be a response to the distortions emerging from political populism and administrative careerism. But such activism acquires credibility only when the institutions of judiciary operate with a measure of transparency. Such credibility is a *sine qua non* for judicial activism to gain acceptability and legitimacy.

Issues of privilege and contempt, of legislators and of the judiciary have long crossed the canons of democracy. The citizens believe that both the legislators and the judiciary are not inclined to codify their ever expanding privileges; this tendency amounts to 'contempt of the citizens' in any republic. The privileges, self proclaimed, almost in a competitive spirit, by the legislative, executive and judicial functionaries are mostly unrelated to their roles and responsibilities. The most vulgar display of these privileges takes place on the streets, in utter contempt of "we the people".

Where functionaries of state misuse, disuse, abuse and distort law , people tend to take law into their own hands; they tend to develop respect for 'people's court' and where the umpiring, elaborately set out by the Constitution, slides or fails, the institutions suffer loss of legitimacy and credibility.This is the social reality in India today. If this trend is not arrested - of which there is not even a mute indication, things do not stagnate, they further slide into extremism of various hues, and intensities in forms such as terrorism. We had several Chief Ministers who had advised citizens to take to arms. In place of social transformation, as designed and proclaimed, we could end up with social turbulence and anarchy.

Extremism

Legislators, administrators and judges buying peace with extremists (of various hues) is an all-India phenomenon today. While leaders seek and secure the support of extremists in order to get elected in some places, elsewhere elected representatives either desert their constituencies or resign from their elected offices out of fear of extremists. Police who are supposed to protect the citizens, wind up their shops from 'extremist' affected areas and move to 'safer' places. While police do not 'enter' the villages as long as the extremists are within the villages, as if a convention of 'safe passage', in some other places police are the informers and suppliers and sellers of weapons to the extremists. These are signs not merely of withdrawal of state, and defeat of democracy, but represent the process of decay of both democracy and the state.

An Agenda for the Ethics Committee of the Lok Sabha

India is the largest democracy - so says the world, and we seem to be enjoying that status, 'quantitatively' so to say. At the advent of 21st century, the entire humanity - the global society appears poised to move in the direction of global democracy.

Shall India merely struggle to retain its quantitative primacy, or aim at qualitative excellence and radiate the 'democratic' ethic all around the globe? Indian society is quintessentially democratic, secular, and egalitarian not because, but inspite of divisive political processes. Political process ought to be the prime-mover of social transformation, engine of the democratic Republic. Fore us to be able to keep our republic, the political process has to gain and retain its legitimacy and credibility. That is the agenda before the Ethics Committee.

The pollution of the political process in the polity is the cardinal cause of declining ethics of the parliamentary process. Hence, ethics within the House cannot be promoted and sustained for as long as the source and the base of legislatures remain polluted. Looked at it from an entirely different angle, who else, if not the legislatures and the legislators, can cleanse the political process and its polluting influences from spreading all over the body politic? We have to quickly convert our quantitative democracy into qualitative democracy. It will be out of place to carve out and elaborate an action plan here. But some of the elements of an agenda for the Ethics Committee can be indicated.

Supremacy of Institutions over Individuals : In the seemingly endless debate over 'individuals versus systems' we need to recognise that individuals have to take the initiative to strengthen the systems; systems and institutions are supreme and individuals are merely and momentarily, instrumental; and trustees in making institutions endure and sustain. Under conditions of democracy, institutions have to be made autonomous, accountable and transparent in order to acquire and retain their legitimacy and credibility.

In a constitutional republic , the three instrumentalities of state are assigned different but complementary roles with common, inseparable objectives, and goals. Such a complementarity and constitutional balance gets disturbed, if not disrupted, when individual functionaries, momentarily occupying positions, tend to arrogate to themselves the attributes of hierarchy and superior - subordinate dispositions. There may be, and will be, situations and instances of intra and inter institutional - conflict which can and should be resolved through democratic conventions and within the framework of constitutional culture, and even more importantly, through creative interaction across the table.

In the Indian experience, one gets the impression that the political leadership has always been inclined to resolve areas of divergence of opinion, and inter institutional conflict, but the judicial leadership has tended to maintain that such conflicts have to be resolved in the court-rooms alone. However, if and when 'creative' dialogues are undertaken, needless to say that the fact of such dialogues must be transparent, so that the citizens do not get an impression that inter-institutional friction and conflict is converted into 'personal-agenda'.

In case of conflict between the elected and appointed executive, the impression is : either there has been a sense of withdrawal, or conflict, or the other extreme of collusion, but not complementarity. The most adverse impact of the process of governance on the democratic republic arises not from the growing conflict between the legislature and the judiciary, but from an utter imbalance in the relationship between the elected and the appointed executive. The mass transfers of senior administrators as much as at the field level (such as Police Station House Officers) almost as the first act after the swearing in of any new Chief Minister has not merely diluted the efficacy of bureaucracy, but even worse, has led to either demoralisation, or total submission to the party in power, with the adjunct consequences of collusion, and partnership in corruption.

Indian democracy suffers disproportionately from conflict between the 'ruling' and 'opposition' parties, as though those 'opposition', constitute the enemies of the country, and the 'ruling' represent the preferred darling of democratic process. The distortions of the political process that are reflected as the 'negative vote' in the electoral process, almost consistently during the first five decades of the republic should make our political leaders think that we need to legitimise and institutionalise the role, status and thus the image of 'opposition' in the legislatures, and in the process of governance. Over a period of time, opposition (and all parties have been in opposition) has started conducting itself as though they have to 'oppose' everything, even the policies that they had carved out while in government. The party/parties in 'power' tend to treat those in 'opposition' as though they are enemies of the nation, and traitors, not recognising that all the parties and their representatives have gone though the 'same' electoral process.

The Ethics Committee of the Parliament has to concern itself, inorder to do justice to itself, with (a) democratic conventions, (b) constitutional propriety and (c) fault-lines of social transformation while setting standards for the complementary tasks of the instrumentalities of state, within the framework of their common, constitutional objectives, and the vision of India.

5

A CASE FOR JUDICIAL ACTIVISM

Sunder Raman

Judicial activism, in fact, has been age old. The proponents of judicial activism take it as normal assertion of judicial power, a part of judicial review authority, result of judicial creativity and the necessary inbuilt mechanism to uphold rule of law and canons of natural justice. For the opponents, judicial activism is a term of abuse. The two sides have their own perceptions; their own reasons, not necessarily independent of their self interests. And, when the two sides overstate their positions, the casualty is objectivity.

Way back, in the early 17th century, Lord Coke, Chief Justice of the Court of Common Pleas was accused of questioning the supremacy of Parliament, when he declared the impugned Act void on the grounds of 'common right and reason' in the historic *Dr. Bonham's case* (year 1610). Interestingly, the case also earned him the title: legal father of judicial review. The same was the fate of Chief Justice Marshall, who expounded the doctrine of judicial review in the famous case of *Marbury v. Madison* in 1803. However, kudos and brick-bats aside, the power of judicial review has firmly remained a part of democratic constitutionalism world over, ever since; occasionally, "it has been resented, evaded and even attacked but never overthrown". Judicial activism is only an extension of judicial review power. In fact, any decision of serious political consequence may be labelled as judicial activism.

Judicial activism, indubitably, is a sharp double edged weapon; it can do immense good and can also produce devastating results.

In 1857, in the *Dred Scott case*, the American Supreme Court declared slaves as a property of slave owners and faced the wrath of the people. If one were to consider it as judicial activism, it was nothing but inhuman judicial activism. Again, in 1930s (1935-36), when the U.S. Supreme Court struck down twelve New Deal statutes, meant to stem the economic rot, it was nothing but retrograde judicial activism. Such decisions produce sharp and violent reactions in the society and the various institutions and agencies demand judicial restraint. In contrast, the American Supreme Court has also had several great judges deeply committed to do justice with an independent and fearless mind. The American apex court has declared in unequivocal terms racial segregation in all its forms unconstitutional, enlarged the authority of Congress to legislate against racial discrimination, expanded the protection of the Bill of Rights to apply to state and local officials, enlarged the scope of political speech, limited the authority of states to regulate obscenity, raised the wall of separation between the church and the state higher and insisted that legislative bodies be apportioned to reflect equal voting power among voters regardless of where they live. These decisions represent the admixture of *juris science* and *juris conscience*.

Indian judiciary also has received its share of brickbats and bouquets. Since independence, the Supreme Court has handed down several landmark judgments; it has defined many legal concepts, has steadily expanded its role, has adopted PIL jurisprudence, has ventured into new areas; and of course, has also given unreasonable and erroneous decisions (who can deny, after all the judges too are human and fallible). Over the years, the Court has dextrously added new dimensions to the rule of law and has successfully devised new techniques to prevent legislative tardiness and executive discretion. It has clearly demonstrated its commitments to participatory justice, just standards of procedures, immediate access to justice and preventive arbitrary state action through *Maneka Gandhi*, *Sunil Batra*, *Bihar Undertrials*, *Punjab Police*, *Bombay Pavement Dwellers*, *Bihar Care Home*, *Francis Coralie cases*, to name a few.

Unlike in the U.S., the singular contribution of introducing PIL in India has come from some of the Supreme Court judges themselves. Though a late-comer in India, PIL has firmly stayed and is being continuously fashioned by the Court. The Public Interest Litigation has been used for providing various types of reliefs to the undertrial prisoners, to ameliorate the conditions in protective homes for women, to prohibit traffic in women, to check custodial violence, for the release of bonded labour, for the enforcement of labour laws, for environment protection and so on. The Indian judiciary through PIL has conveyed the solemn message to all the instrumentalities of governance that it cannot stand idly by, particularly when there is abuse of power and misgovernance.

> ***Unlike in the U.S., the singular contribution of introducing PIL in India has come from some of the Supreme Court judges themselves. Though a late-corner in India, PIL has firmly stayed and is being continuously fashioned by the Court. The Public Interest Litigation has been used for providing various types of reliefs to the undertrial prisoners, to ameliorate the conditions in protective homes for women, to prohibit traffic in women, to check custodial violence, for the release of bonded labour, for the enforcement of labour laws, for environment protection and so on. The Indian judiciary through PIL has conveyed the solemn message to all the instrumentalities of governance that it cannot stand idly by, particularly when there is abuse of power and misgoverance.***

Some of the recent judgments of the Supreme Court include enhanced payment for the women widowed in November 1984 anti-Sikh riots (additional Rs.3.3 lacs), invalidation of arbitrary decisions of former Congress Ministers in allotting government accommodation, shops, petrol pumps and gas agencies, and asking the errant ministers to recompense the government by paying heavy sum from their personal accounts, issuing of instructions to the CBI as to how they should go about investigating various scams, immediate closure of unlicensed veneer, plywood and saw mills in Maharashtra and Uttar Pradesh to check large scale destruction of forests in the two States, etc. The high and mighty have been arraigned in court for thievery, fraud and similar contemptible charges. This new ethos is obviously very disturbing for the political elites; it is just not acceptable to them. They have already initiated a move to curb PIL ostensibly to help clear the backlog and restrain judicial populism or judicial over-activism. The proposed PIL Bill will require a forfeitable deposit of Rs. one lakh along with public interest petition barring the ones filed by or on behalf of a poor person. Who is a poor person? A person earning less than Rs.6,000/-, defines the draft bill. It is a case of sheer desperation. The votaries of the Bill need to be reminded that the right to move a PIL is an integral part of articles 32 and 226; even a constitutional amendment to impair or abrogate this right may not stand judicial scrutiny on the basis of the basic structure limitation. PIL, 'a wonder drug' for the aggrieved common man cannot be taken away. Come to think of it, it is not judicial activism, it is judicial redressal.

So far the misuse of PIL is concerned, judiciary has already evolved an effective mechanism to throw out dubious cases. As Dr. Rajeev Dhavan has pointed out : "the court monitors PIL cases *in extenso*; and has made it clear that there is no fundamental right to have a PIL case heard." Thus, judiciary steps in only when required. Let there be rule of law and democratic governance, the judicial pendulum will automatically swing the other way.

6

JUDICIAL ACTIVISM

Misdirected Exercise

S.D. Bali

Legislature, Executive and Judiciary are the three independent and separate wings in parliamentary democracy. Their spheres of operation and areas of action are clearly defined. But unfortunately the operators of the system are so much obsessed by ambitions of supremacy that each wing is eager and anxious to oversmart others and tries to arrogate to itself the role, powers and-onging to it.

Unchecked entry of criminals and undesirable elements in the legislatures have eroded the sanctity and authority of these institutions to effectively oversee the functioning of the executive to keep it within limits. The executive, instead of enforcing the rule of law is engaged in encouraging corruption and protecting the corrupt, bringing peril to national pride. Judiciary - the only hope in such peculiar circumstances - is also going astray. When it first asserted, its over-activism proved counter productive. Judicious thinking and approach is tested when situations demand the application of the rule of law on self. Here the judiciary faltered if not failed. When it came to their own appointments and transfers, the word "consultation" by the government in this context was interpreted by the apex court as their "concurrence" so that they themselves decide the selection of their brother judges.

Under the provisions of the Constitution as also as a matter of propriety, precedent and convention, the President acts on the advice of the Council of Ministers. The appointments/ transfers of the judges of Supreme Court/high courts are made accordingly. The recommendations are made in consultation with the respective chief justices and this "consultation" as per the Supreme Court verdict means "concurrence". More clearly it means that Judiciary has the final say and the executive is merely a channel to pass on judiciary's proposal as its own advice even if it does not agree with it. If, however, the executive is adamant and not keen to go by the recommendations of the judiciary, a stalemate would be inevitable, bringing all the attendant unpleasant corollaries. It is a well-known fact that "will" of the people is represented in the legislature through their elected representatives who constitute the executive and the legislature and not through the judges who are the appointees of the executive. The people being "sovereign", their "will" must prevail. The dictum that the king (the executive in the changed system of governance) does no wrong is no more relevant in a parliamentary democracy. Legislations are passed, implemented, amended and even scrapped. Similarly in the judiciary, judgments by the courts are reviewed, modified and even reversed, majority and minority views are reflected to meet the ends of justice. The saying about the Mughals that "*Har Keh Aamad Imarat-E-Nau Sakhat*" (whosoever came built a new building) aptly applies to the political parties - the modern version of the old system. Immediately after coming to power every party is interested to amend, change or alter the laws and orders of the out-going party in a bid to leave their own imprint. But, in the process of rapid political changes, nobody's stamp lasts.

> ***A constitutional amendment bill was drafted and approved by the Cabinet for being introduced in the Parliament, to change the present system where the concurrence of the chief justices was necessary for judicial appointments and transfers and to restore the power of selection and appointment of the judges to the executive. But even after having been listed in the list of business, it was withheld for unexplained reasons. Whatever may be the case, the motivation behind the move is clearly to have a committed and compliant judiciary.***

It is perhaps in this backdrop and irked by judicial activism which has put the executive in the dock and on the defensive, that the government is now using the legislature to clip the wings of the judiciary. A constitutional amendment bill was drafted and approved by the Cabinet for being introduced in the Parliament, to change the present system where the concurrence of the chief justices was necessary for judicial appointments and transfers and to restore the power of selection and appointment of the judges to the executive. But' even after having been listed in the list of business, it was withheld for unexplained reasons. Whatever may be the case, the motivation behind the move is clearly to have a committed and compliant judiciary.

In the circumstances, only two options are left to tide over the peculiar situation. One is to implement the recommendations of Dinesh Goswami Committee for the establishment of a Judicial Commission to oversee the appointments/transfer of the Supreme Court and High Court judges and the second is that the whole thing should be left to the wisdom of the President of India who may consider all viewpoints and recommendations and take final decision. The procedure for removal of judges also needs to be reviewed in the changed political scenario of coalition governments. The power for removal of a judge should also be vested in the Judicial Commission or the President as the case may be. Then alone would the independence and impartiality or the judiciary be ensured.

7

CONSTITUTION AND JUDICIAL ACTIVISM

Independence of Judiciary and Politics of Appointments

Nafees Ahmad

Ever since the evolution of civilization and its graduation to modernity, human existence has moved from police state to welfare state. Republican values emanating from concepts like the rule of law, judicial review and independence of the judiciary are cherished in any modern democratic polity wedded to good governance.

The doctrine of constitutionalism as enshrined in the Constitution of India envisages a welfare state where the state is expected to generate programmes for providing quality life and social security to its people through legislation and administrative action.

In recent years, a new class of litigation has developed which is propelled by a social agenda of human rights. It is known as Public Interest Litigation (PIL). It became possible as a result of what has come to be called judicial activism exercised by the Supreme Court and High Courts under articles 32 and 226 of the Constitution. PIL is a modern legal mechanism for redressal of grievances in a welfare state. It is less expensive and more efficacious in matters of transgressions and circumventions of rights of the people against governmental instrumentality and public authority.

This exercise of "judicial activism" in an age of human rights, is virtually a product of executive inaction. The term "judicial activism" is a misnomer because judiciary is only discharging its constitutional obligations duly mandated under articles 32 (citizens' right to constitutional remedies) 226 (power of high courts to issue certain writs) and 137 (review of judgements or orders by the Supreme Court, 140 (ancillary powers of Supreme Court) and 141 (Law declared by Supreme Court to be binding on all courts) of the Constitution of India.

Earlier, judgements and decrees were passed and files were closed and shelved. The present judiciary is following a more pragmatic technique of "Judgements with Monitoring". Today, not only are judgements pronounced but their result-oriented implementation is also ensured through new tools, methods and techniques. Today, government officials are asked to submit their progress reports pertaining to matters *sub-judice* at every stage till the case is finally adjudicated upon. This pious "constitutional judicial alertness" is seen as "judicial activism".

In fact, judicial activism is that legal process by which relief is provided to the disadvantaged and aggrieved party. Thus, where there is a gap in legislation or law is silent on a specific point and an eventuality of needing prompt redressal arises, Union judiciary exercises its inherent powers by virtue of being a custodian and watchdog of the Constitution. It becomes imperative on the part of the apex court of the land to fill up this legislative gap because Parliament could not have envisioned future exigencies and extraordinary situations.

Moreover, the concepts of state and sovereignty have been considerably diluted under the universal scheme of human rights where national boundaries are losing their meaning and an individual is being regarded as a subject of international law. In this conspectus international human rights conventions are also getting due respect in municipal legal systems.

The Supreme Court while entertaining PILs is also discharging its social responsibility without prejudices and predilections. Recent judicial pronouncements have paved the way for the institutionalization of individual accountability in a democratic governance. By way of PILs, problems like child labour, bounded labour, housing, illegal detention of undertrials, custodial deaths, environmental pollution, protection to and preservation of historical monuments and violation of human rights have been greatly mitigated at the fag end of the 20th century.

On the other hand, public interest litigation is being misused for populism by some individuals and non-governmental organisations (NGOs) which is detrimental to the very purpose of this mechanism. The Supreme Court should not entertain every public interest petition; only real and genuine issues need be remedied by resorting to the public interest litigation technique because otherwise, our apex court may be blamed for its "over activism" which may turn into judicial terrorism.

> ***The Supreme Court should not entertain every public interest petition; only real and genuine issues need be remedied by resorting to the public interest litigation technique because otherwise, our apex court may be blamed for its "over activism" which may turn into judicial terrorism.***

An independent judiciary is the soul of a parliamentary democractic dispensation of governance. Political parties are unfortunately bent upon to reverse the existing mechanism by which the appointments of judges are made to the Supreme Court and the High Courts. In the wake of the development of Public Interest Litigation (PIL) which is a rare Indian contribution to world jurisprudence, Supreme Court of India today has become the strongest apex Court of the world. It became possible only because "primacy" was accorded to the "opinion" of the Chief Justice of India in the appointment of judges.

> ***A corrupt politician who holds a public office encourages corruption. It percolates to the lowest rungs of the system. Our country is paying a heavy price for the nefarious and sinister designs of the politicians who act in connivance with the criminals. The report of the Vohra Committee must be implemented in toto because the common man is already tired of the malaise that has gripped our polity.***

It was the judicial impact of the highest judiciary that disignated TADA Judge S.N. Dhingra delivered an honest judicial pronouncement and made history by slapping 10 years' rigorous imprisonment coupled with fine on former Union minister and sitting MP Kalpnath Rai for harbouring notorious mafia don Dawood Ibrahim's henchmen. A corrupt politician who holds a public office encourages corruption. It percolates to the lowest rungs of the system. Our country is paying a heavy price for the nefarious and sinister designs of the politicians who act in connivance with the criminals. The report of the Vohra Committee must be implemented in toto because the common man is already tired of the malaise that has gripped our polity.

Ever since the Hawala scam surfaced on the Indian political scene and subsequent political developments took place, politicians have been facing a catena of legal labyrinth which swept the ground from under their feet. Majority of the politicians from different political parties are involved in various scams meaning thereby, they are ganged up against the judiciary and have made common cause for pruning the constitutional wings of one of the important organs of the state in the name of reforming the administration of justice in India. They are afraid of judicial honesty of the justice system. In this connection certain instances of recent political behaviour of these parties may be highlighted.

First, politicians tried to get themselves out of the purview of the Prevention of Corruption Act (PCA) on the ground that MPs & MLAs and Ministers do not come within the definition of public servant. They inconclusively debated the issue in Parliament. They attacked judicial activism but entire exercise of saving their thick skin from the long arms of law failed.

Secondly, Union Law Minister Dr. Rama Kant Khalup wanted to pilot a Public Interest Litigation Bill providing for a prohibitive amount of fee as the cost of litigation. But Khalup could not succeed as this obnoxious move was strongly opposed by the left political constituents of the United Front Government.

> ***Government started the politics of appointment of judges again with the same motive of scuttling any inquiry against them. They behave like modern feudal lords and see judiciary as an impediment in their quest of amassing wealth which is always disproportionate to their known sources of income.***

Even if Parliament had passed the PIL Bill, it could be set aside by the Supreme Court under its power of Judicial Review provided in article 137 as it amounts to the violation of the basic structure of the Constitution envisaged in the Preamble which can not be amended in exercise of the power under article 368 of the Constitution. Preamble of the Constitution of India attached the greatest value to Justice in its different forms such as social, economic and political.

Government started the politics of appointment of judges again with the same motive of scuttling any inquiry against them. They behave like modern feudal lords and see judiciary as an impediment in their quest of amassing wealth which is always disproportionate to their known sources of income.

An independent judiciary shoulders a crucial responsibility in a parliamentary democracy. In this conspectus, Constitution of India provides a detailed regime of provisions with regard to the appointments of judges to Supreme Court and High Courts under articles 124 and 217 respectively. Article 124 (2) stipulates that "every judge of the Supreme Court shall be appointed by the President after consultation with such of the judges of the Supreme Court and of the High Courts in the State as the President may deem necessary for the purpose provided that in the case of appointment of a judge other than the Chief Justice, the Chief Justice of India shall always be consulted. Further article 124 (4) provides that "a judge of the Supreme Court shall not be removed from his office except by an order of the President passed after an address by each House of Parliament supported by a majority of the total membership of that House and by a majority of not less than two thirds of the members of that House present and voting, has been presented to the President in the same session for such removal on the ground of proved misbehaviour or incapacity. In addition to this, it would be the duty of the Parliament to regulate the procedure by law for the investigation and proof of the misbehaviour or incapacity of a judge.

Judges to the High Courts under article 217 (1) are to be appointed by the President having consulted with the Chief Justice of India, the Governor of the State and, in the case of appointment of a judge other than the Chief Justice, the Chief Justice of the High Court. A judge of High Court may also be removed from his office by the President in the same manner as provided in clause (4) of article 124 for the removal of a judge of the Supreme Court.

The word "consultation" has always been of contention between the executive and the judiciary. What does it imply? Does it mean concurrence of the apex judiciary headed by Chief Justice of India? What is the nature of consultation? These are the questions of utmost importance agitating the judicial minds in the country.

These questions came before the Union judicial establishment on two different occasions. Firstly, in the case of *Union of India V. Sankalchand Seth* in 1977 and, secondly, in the case of *S.P. Gupta*

V. Union of India in 1982 which is popularly known as *Judges Transfer Case* where it was adjudicated upon by the Supreme Court that word "consultation" does not mean "concurrence" of the Chief Justice of India but it must be effective and imply exchange of views after examining the merits. But in 1993, a nine judge Constitution Bench of the Supreme Court in a landmark judgment in the case of *Supreme Court Advocates-on-Record Association V. Union of India* held that in matters of appointment and transfer of judges of the Supreme Court and High Courts, Chief Justice of India shall have the final say having consulted his colleagues and seniority shall be the sole criterion for the appointment of the Chief Justice of India. While overruling its earlier decision in S.P. Gupta's case where it was held that the executive (central government) had the final authority in appointments and transfer of judges, the Court stated that the opinion of the Chief Justice of India should have the greatest weight in the selection of judges in which the executive functions as a check on selection process exercised by the Chief Justice of India. Justice Verma delivered the majority judgement and observed : "Thus, the executive element in the appointment process has been reduced to minimum and political influence is eliminated. It is for this reason that the word "consultation" instead of "concurrence" was used in the Constitution but that was done merely to indicate that absolute discretion was not given to any one, not even to the Chief Justice of India as an individual, much less to the executive."

We must have a cursory glance retrospectively on the politics of appointments from 1973 onwards. The year 1973 catapulated the principle of seniority into a political quandry when then Prime Minister Late Mrs. Indira Gandhi appointed A.N Ray as Chief Justice of India superseding three of the senior colleagues, Justice Shelat, Hegde, and Grover by taking advantage of Law Commission's Report of 1956 handed down by then Attorney-General M.C Setalvad who castigated seniority practice as the sole criterion to be qualified for the top slot in the judicial hierarchy. Setalvad recommended experience, administrative competence and merit of a person as a judge to be appointed as Chief Justice of India. Mrs. Gandhi exploited 1956 Law Commission Report for her political survival within few hours of the delivery of the judgment in the famous Fundamental Rights case. Subsequently, these three eminent judges of the Supreme Court laid their offices down. The action of the Government raised a great polemical debate in the country. It is distressing to note that we could not establish viable and healthy constitutional conventions despite having spent fifty years of independence. Although, we have a written Constitution but everything can not be written. In a constitutional democracy institutions are higher than the individuals howsoever honest, upright and important they may be.

Again, Law Commission of India submitted its 121st Report in July, 1987 and aptly concluded that "everyone is agreed that the present scheme or model or mechanism for recruitment to superior judiciary has failed to deliver the goods because political considerations have entered the process of selection of judges."

The Law Commission of India recommended the installation of a broad based National Judicial Service Commission consisting of various interests such as judicial, political, social and constitutional. Although judiciary got some respite in 1993 when primacy was given to the opinion of the Chief Justice of India, political citadel in country again started with a new vigour to cut judiciary to size.

Whatever may be the form and shape of the proposed Commission, "primacy" must be accorded to the opinion of the Chief Justice of India and "individual judicial accountability" must also be evolved as is the case with executive and legislature so that exceptional matters of judicial corruption could also be contained. However, it is legislative corruption which inbreeds every kind of corruption and engulfs vital and major institutions in a constitutional governance.

> ***The best way out of the present situation is that the National Judicial Service Commission should be entrusted with the power of selection and transfer of the judges. Moreover, the Commission must also set up a Judicial Performance Committee modelled on the basis of Judicial Performance Commission of the United States of America.***

The best way out of the present situation is that the National Judicial Service Commission should be entrusted with the power of selection and transfer of the judges. Moreover, the Commission must also set up a Judicial Performance Committee modelled on the basis of Judicial Performance Commission of the United States of America. The Report of the Judicial Performance Committee should be tabled in the Houses of Parliament and if a judge is found unfit, proceedings should be initiated for removal of the judge in accordance with the existing mechanism provided in the Constitution.

8

THE OTHER SIDE OF AN ACTIVE JUDICIARY

Niranjan Sahoo

Judiciary is in a hurry. Believe or not within a short span our judiciary has acquired the new found status-savior without call, our esteemed judges as crusaders at will, and the wise or otherwise legal community as the prophets of the doom. Consciously or unconsciously, all of them forget that they are no saints, no less irresponsible as the legislature and the executive. Earlier the judiciary used to examine the validity of an act, now it provides dictums how to make an act, how to best protect environment, where to relocate polluted industries, where to dump garbage, how best Cauvery water can be distributed, and how should a Prime Minister function ? It all sounds like a government by judiciary is very much on the cards.

The judiciary has its tale of woe. Our legal system is wooden, archaic and cumbersome. The prevailing procedures and practices are the by-products of certain basic enactments which are out dated. Like the Indian Evidence Act of 1872 and Civil Procedure Code of 1908. After the admission of petitions, follow service of summons, filing of documents, verification of witnesses, submission of arguments by lawyers, writing of judgments and sanctioning the final orders. Each stage is a painful journey and its implementation can take its own course. Millions of cases are pending. Often cases extend beyond the life time of the original litigant. This had prompted Justice Bhagwati to declare in the eighties that "our judicial system is almost on the verge of collapse."

At a time when corruption has acquired the magnitude of a national calamity, the judiciary is not far behind in this respect from other organs. The cases of corruption against four judges of Bombay High Court in 1990, the controversy relating to Justice Ramaswamy of Supreme Court, are some of the glaring instances of the other side of an active judiciary. Particularly, at the lower level in some parts of the country the integrity of judiciary has become increasingly suspect. May be this can be excused since in our society, fictious rationally and fatalistic psyche, corruption is fast becoming institutionalized as a way of life. The judges are after all human beings drawn from the same society where we all live. Not all the judges are philosopher kings. While the judiciary is advising all other branches to adopt the policy of decentralization so as to avoid delay and blockage to perform better, we have got one of the most powerful apex courts in the world which is structurally pyramidical.

Our courts already in arrears have been flooded with new Public Interest Litigation (PIL) on relatively trivial grievances, real or imaginary. The provisions of PIL have been misused by the so called public spirited individuals. There has for instance been litigation to block India's entry into the World Trade Organization (WTO), to impose restricted labour practices, to remove state governments under article 356 and to remove the Prime Minister and the Home Minister. In most of the cases, PIL have been filed by the activists for personal benefit by using the rights of the poor as masks in such campaigns. It is here justice S.R. Pandhian remarked that "these public spirited individuals wear the mask of public interest and file vexatious and frivolous petitions." The most worrisome fact is that yeilding to temptation, the courts are drawn into positive policy-making role, substituting their own policy choices for those of the people's elected representatives. And if in case judges go wrong, who will judge them?

Obviously, here comes the question of judicial accountability. Though the dominant public opinion is in favour of judicial activism, the judges themselves cannot behave as if they were above all criticism or accountability. Such immunity from public scrutiny could lead to misuse of power. It is felt by some that the judges are behaving as if they are more equal than others — just as till yesterday, politicians used to. But if accountability is sought to be enforced on the elected representatives, how about the judiciary? The recent spurt in PIL in variety of situations, the court's quickness to hear them, relaxing procedural bottlenecks, did increase access to justice while on the other hand it has unknowingly hijacked the accountability from the executive. In such cases when the courts are grabbing jurisdiction from the legislature and the executive by taking decisions on their behalf, automatically it is the judiciary which is accountable for its decisions. However, the law-making power (as it is called) of the judiciary is never categorically mentioned in the Constitution and therefore may prove undemocratic and would go against the spirit of the constitution. Though the Indian judiciary has a proud tradition of upholding rule of law and enaoling constitutional governance even during very difficult periods, yet a few lapses in judgments may put a big question mark on judicial accountability.

It is not clear whether this/is because of the complex character and vastness of the Indian state or the structural distortion in the judiciary? The way the Supreme Court handled the medical college admission and the Mandal controversy was unfortunate. Both were very important issues affecting the lives of large section. These were matters for legislative action. Once the courts took cognizance of these, it became the target customer of all sorts of socio-politically sensitive but unresolved issues. This urge to correct injustice led the courts to uncharted sphere of governance in which judicial intervention was perhaps not adequately matched with judicial restraint and foresight.

Besides the courts, the whole legal community plays a crucial role in the process of accountability. The judges are drawn from among the lawyers who have the background of the bar. In all cases of delay in litigation or politicization of the judicial process, the legal profession plays a vital or decisive role. To cite one instance, in *Satish Sharma's case* the Supreme Court declared that "it is high time the public servant should be held responsible personally for his *malafide* acts in the discharge of their functions as public servants." If that is the case, the judges are also public servants under Section-21 of the Indian Penal Code. They cannot escape accountability. There should be appropriate mechanisms to deal with the arbitrary, corrupt and dishonest judges from all branches.

The story of judicial overactivism does not end here. There is a hot debate going round on the issue of contempt of court. Ordinarily, the contempt provision should be used sparingly and as a last resort. Of late, the contempt power of the court is being used even on lesser or petty cases. Legally, the court has the power to punish someone in case of disobedience of its directive (Article 142). Yet its frequent use including in minor cases will bring down the purpose of the clause. The higher courts say, that incase of contempt of court truth or justification of action cannot be pleaded as a defence. Truth is no defence is a law made by the judges themselves. It is neither God-given nor one flowing from the Constitution. Even the U.S. court where from we have borrowed this, merely decides the constitutional validity of an act and stops there. May be this has gone unnoticed by our courts.

If the above are true, the judiciary cannot claim for itself the virtues of infallibility. This is to state that in the process of arbitrating the grievances of the common man, the judiciary has travelled too far unto the point of making it a super executive. The governance of the country is a serious matter and cannot be carried out by a great judiciary alone. Intervention into others' domain would gradually take the prophets of doom to the point of no return. May be the judiciary is yet to experience the risks of playing non-zero-sum game. What is needed is a new vision, not correction of a faulty vision. If necessity is the mother of invention, then the crisis we now face must be the mother of structural and systematic reform and action. We must aim at preventing future generations from inheriting our past as their future. The time has come for judiciary to undertake some rethinking and self-analysis before it becomes too late.

9

JUDICIARY-LEGISLATURE INTERFACE

Subhash C. Kashyap

In a democracy, sovereignty must vest in the people and ideally the people should govern themselves. But, with the growing complexities of governance and the size of the nation states, direct democracy of the type of Greek city states or the Indian village republics of ancient times, is no more feasible. Also, sovereignty in the hands of the people is an abstraction. In order to become exercisable, this sovereignty has to be institutionalised. The very first and the most fundamental application of their sovereignty by the people is in giving to themselves a Constitution. The Constitution establishes the main organs of the State - the legislature, the executive and the judiciary - defines their powers, delimits their jurisdictions, demarcates their responsibilities and regulates their relationships with each other and with the people. Every institution of the State is expected to be functional and active in discharging its duties in the sphere assigned to it by the Constitution.

However, the traditional concept of the legislature making laws, executive executing or implementing the laws and the judiciary adjudicating disputes and interpreting the laws and the Constitution, no more holds good. In modern parliamentary political science and jurisprudence, roles and functions of the three organs of the State overlap, interact with each other and are interlinked. Law-making is neither the only nor the major job of a legislature today. Also, law making is no more the exclusive preserve of the legislature; there are many other actors in the drama of legislation and judiciary is also one of the leading players. Instead of the separate faces of the legislature and the judiciary, their interface, therefore, assumes greater significance.

Secondly, when we think of legislature-judiciary interface, we need to remember that in a parliamentary polity, executive also is a part of the legislature. It comes out of the legislature, remains responsible to it and exercises powers of governance only on its behalf.

The Constitution of India embodies a federal structure *inter alia* with powers of legislation divided between the Union Parliament and State Legislatures. However, it the High Courts and the Supreme Court set up by the Constitution as parts of an independent judiciary, form a single integrated judicial structure with jurisdiction over all laws - Union, State, Civil, Criminal or Constitutional. Unlike the U.S., we do not have separate federal and State Court systems. The entire judiciary is one hierarchy of courts. It not only adjudicates disputes and acts as the custodian of individual rights and freedoms but may from time to time need to interpret the Constitution and review legislation to determine its vires *vis-a-vis* the Constitution. The word of the Supreme Court is the final law of the land unless its interpretation is reviewed or reversed by the Supreme Court itself or the law or the Constitution is suitably amended by Parliament. The Supreme Court also functions as the arbiter of any disputes in regard to jurisdiction and distribution of powers between the States or between the Union and the States.

Under the scheme of the Constitution, Parliament and the Judiciary come into contact with each other in many ways.

Constitution and Powers of Courts

Parliament has the power to make laws regulating the constitution, organisation, jurisdiction and powers of the Courts. It was laid down in the Constitution that the number of judges other than the Chief Justice would not be more than seven. The Parliament was, however, empowered to prescribe a larger number of Judges by law (article 124) under this provision, it has been possible for Parliament to raise the number of judges to 25.

Parliament may by law:

i. Extend the jurisdiction of a High Court to, or exclude the jurisdiction of a High Court from, any Union territory;

ii. establish a common High Court for two or more States or for two or more States and a Union territory; and

iii. constitute a High Court for a Union territory or declare any Court in any such territory to be a High Court for all or any of the purposes of the Constitution (article 241).

Appointment of Judges

All the judges of the Supreme Court and of the High Courts are to be appointed by the President after consultation with such of the judges of the Supreme Court and of the High Courts as he may deem fit. The position as it has crystallized is that in case of vacancy in the position of the Chief Justice of India, the senior most judge of the Supreme Court must be appointed. In case of all other judges, the Chief Justice of India along with his two senior most colleagues should have a decisive voice.

Removal of Judges

According to the latest reports, however, attempts are now being made by the government to assert its rights in the matter of appointment and transfer of judges and for the purpose it is proposed to amend the Constitution.

A judge of the Supreme Court or any High Court can be removed from his office by the President, only if a joint address passed by both Houses of Parliament with a special majority (*i.e.*, by a majority of the total membership of the House and by a majority of not less than two-thirds of the members of each House present and voting) is presented to him (article 124(4) and 218).

It may be very exphatically clarified here that contrary to the common belief, there is no provision for impeachment of a judge in the Constitution. There are fundamental differences between the concept of impeachment and the procedure for removal provided in the Constitution.

Parliament is not empowered to discuss the conduct of any Judge of the Supreme Court or of a High Court in the discharge of his duties except in the case of a motion for presenting an address to the President praying for the removal of a Judge (article 121).

Incidentally, it may be very exphatically clarified here that contrary to the common belief, there is no provision for impeachment of a judge in the Constitution. There are fundamental differences between the concept of impeachment and the procedure for removal provided in the Constitution.

Barring of Court Jurisdiction

Parliament may by law provide for the establishment of an administrative tribunal for the Union and a separate administrative tribunal for each State or for two or more States. The law made under the provision may specify the jurisdiction and powers of the tribunals. Such law may exclude the jurisdiction of all Courts, except the jurisdiction of the Supreme Court under article 136, with respect of certain specified matters (articles 323A and 323B). Further, the Constitution empowers Parliament to create an all-India judicial service which shall not include any post inferior to that of a district judge (articles 312(1) and (3)).

The validity of any proceedings in either House of Parliament cannot be questioned before a court of law on the ground of any alleged irregularity of procedure (articles 122(1) and 212(1)). The presiding officer of each House or any other officer or Member of Parliament who is for the time being vested with the powers to regulate procedure, or to enforce or carry out the decisions of either House of Parliament, is not subject to the jurisdiction of the courts in exercise of those powers (articles 122(2) and 105(3)).

No member of Parliament is liable to any proceedings in any court in respect of anything said or any vote given by him in Parliament or any committee thereof. Also, publication of any report, paper, votes or proceedings of Parliament by or under authority of a House of Parliament is protected against any court proceedings (articles 105(2) and 194(2)).

Judicial Review

Courts in India are endowed with powers of judicial review of legislation. But, if an Act of Parliament is set aside by the judiciary as *ultra vires* or violative of the Constitution, Parliament can re enact it after removing the defects for which it was set aside. Also, Parliament may, within the limits of its constituent powers, amend the Constitution in such a manner that the law no longer remains unconstitutional. Thus, the Parliament in India is not as sovereign as the British Parliament where no judicial review of legislation is permitted. At the same time, the judiciary in India is not as supreme as in the United States of America which recognises virtually no limit on the scope of judicial review and the pronouncement of the Supreme Court in regard to the legality of a legislative is final. India has adopted a middle course and a compromise between the British sovereignty of Parliament and American Judicial Supremacy. Since we have a written Constitution and the powers and functions of every organ are defined and delimited by the Constitution, there is no question of any organ - not even Parliament - being sovereign. Both Parliament and the Supreme Court are supreme in their respective spheres.

Incorporation of a Chapter on Fundamental Rights in the Constitution of India makes judicial review specially relevant. Article 12 guarantees Fundamental Rights against all State action. And 'State' under this article has been defined to include the Government and Parliament of India and the Government and the Legislature of each of the States and all local or other authorities within the territory of India or under the control of the Government.

Anti-Defection Law

The Constitution (52nd Amendment) Act, 1985 amended articles 101, 102, 190 and 191 of the Constitution regarding vacation of seats and disqualification from membership of Parliament and the State Legislatures and added a new schedule (10th Schedule) to the Constitution setting out certain provisions as to disqualification of members on grounds of defection. The 10th Schedule *inter alia* provided that all proceedings in relation to any question as to disqualification of a member of a House under the Schedule would be deemed to be proceedings in Parliament within the meaning of article 122 or, as the case may be, proceedings in the Legislature of a State within the meaning of article 122; and notwithstanding anything in the Constitution, no court will have any jurisdiction in respect of any matter connected with the disqualification of a member of a House.

The Anti-Defection Law, has been the subject matter of a controversy from the very beginning. It has been questioned on several grounds, *viz.* that it is violative of the basic structure of the Constitution, that it is beyond the competence of Parliament, and that it gives preference to expediency over principles. The Paragraph which barred the jurisdiction of the courts was struck down as being *ultra vires* of the Constitution by the High Court of Punjab and Haryana. When an appeal against this order was preferred, the Supreme Court found that there were legal infirmities in the passage of the Anti-Defection Law inasmuch as the Constitution Amendment Bill had not been ratified by the requisite number of State Assemblies before being presented for the President's assent. Also, the Speaker's functions under the 10th Schedule called for a judicial determination of issues under the law and the process of determining the question of disqualification could not be considered part of the proceedings of the House and as such not amenable to judicial review. The Supreme Court struck down Para 7 of the Schedule barring the jurisdiction of Courts and declared that while operating under the Anti-Defection Law, the Speaker was in the position of a tribunal and therefore his decisions like those of all tribunals were subject to judicial review.

Two other areas in which the judiciary and the legislature have in recent years come into close contact with each other have been the issue of parliamentary privileges and the imposition of President's rule in the States.

The Constitution makers did envisage codification of privileges by law and Parliament has been avoiding doing so to avoid being subjected to judicial review and scrutiny. The Press and the citizens would naturally like to have greater transparency and to know what precisely are the privileges. For this, earlier these are codified the better.

Parliamentary Privileges

Article 105 of the Constitution provides for the powers, privileges etc. of the Houses of Parliament and of the members and committees thereof. The corresponding article for State legislatures is article 194. The basic law is that all citizens including members of Parliament should be treated equally before the law. They have the same rights and liberties as ordinary citizens except when they perform their duties in Parliament. The privileges are available to the members only when and to the extent that they are functioning as representatives of the people in Parliament and discharging their parliamentary responsibilities. The privileges do not, in any way, exempt the members from their normal obligations to society which apply to them as much and perhaps more closely in that capacity, as they apply to others. Also, the purpose of the people, through the Constitution, granting to Members certain privileges is only to enable the latter to serve the people without any hinderance. Ideally, these should never be allowed to degenerate into a conflict between the privileges of Members against the rights of the citizens.

It has been held by the Supreme Court in the Searchlight case that the freedom of speech conferred on members under article 105 is subject only to those provisions of the Constitution which regulate the procedure of Parliament and to the rules and standing orders of the House, but is free from any restrictions which may be imposed by any law made under article 19(2) upon the freedom of speech of an ordinary citizen. Any investigation outside Parliament in respect of anything said or done by members in the discharge of their parliamentary duties would amount to a serious interference with the members' rights. Even though a speech delivered by a member in the House may amount to contempt of court, no action can be taken against him in any court. A court, being an outside authority, does not have the power to investigate the matter. Article 122 specifically forbids any inquiry by courts into proceedings of Parliament.

The courts of law in India have thus recognised that a House of Parliament or a State Legislature is the sole authority to judge as to whether or not there has been a breach of privilege in a particular case. It has also been held that the power of the House to commit for contempt is identical with that of the House of Commons and that a court of law would be incompetent to scrutinise the exercise of that power.

The immunity from external influence or interference, however, does not mean an unrestricted licence of speech within the walls of Parliament. It is important to remember that the privileges of the Houses and members and committees thereof are subject to other provisions of the Constitution being construed harmoniously. Thus, for example, the privilege of freedom of speech in Parliament will be subject to rules of procedure framed by Houses of Parliament under article 118 and article 121 forbids discussion in Parliament on the conduct of judges except on a motion for their removal (*M.S. Sharma v. Sri Krishna Sinha*, AIR 1959 SC 395).

In 1965, the Supreme Court in its advisory opinion in Special Reference Case of 1964, (Keshav Singh's case), observed as follows:

It would not be correct to read the majority decision in the *Searchligh case* as laying down a general proposition that whenever there is a conflict between the provisions of the latter part of article 194(3) and any of the provisions of the Fundamental Rights guaranteed by Part III, the latter must yield to the former. The majority decision, therefore, must be taken to have settled that article 19(1)(a) would not apply, and article 21 would.

In dealing with the effect of the provisions contained in clause (3) of article 194, whenever it appears that there is a conflict between the said provisions and the provisions pertaining to Fundamental Rights, an attempt will have to be made to resolve the said conflict by the adoption of the rule of harmonious construction.

The Allahabad High Court, in their judgement in Keshav Singh's case dated 10 March 1965 (*i.e.* delivered after the advisory opinion of the Supreme Court), observed as follows:

i. In our opinion, both upon authority and upon a consideration of the relevant provisions of the Constitution, it must be held that the Legislative Assembly has, by virtue of article 194(3), the same power to commit for its contempt as the House of Commons has.

ii. In our opinion, the provisions of article 22(2) of the Constitution cannot apply to a detention in pursuance of a conviction and imposition of a sentence of imprisonment by competent authority.

iii. Since we have already held that the Legislative Assembly has the power to commit the petitioner for its contempt and since the Legislative Assembly has framed rules for the procedure and conduct of its business under article 208(1), the commitment and deprivation of the personal liberty of the petitioner cannot but be held to be according to the procedure laid down by law within the meaning of article 21 of the Constitution.

iv. Once we come to the conclusion that the Legislative Assembly has the power and jurisdiction to commit for its contempt and to impose the sentence passed on the petitioner, we cannot go into the question of the correctness, propriety or legality of the commitment. This Court cannot, in a petition under article 226 of the Constitution, sit in appeal over the decision of the Legislative Assembly committing the petitioner for its contempt. The Legislative Assembly is the master of its own procedure and is the sole judge of the question whether its contempt has been committed or not.

The Government, therefore, decided that an amendment of the Constitution was not necessary. It was of the opinion that the Legislatures and the Judiciary would develop their own conventions in the light of the opinion given by the Supreme Court and the judgement pronounced by the Allahabad High Court. It may, therefore, be seen that the judgement of the Supreme Court in the Searchlight case is final till today insofar as matters of privilege are concerned.

Article 105(3) of the Constitution stipulates that, apart from the privileges mentioned in the Constitution itself, Parliament may, from time to time, define its privileges by law. No law, however, has so far been enacted by Parliament in pursuance of this provision to define the powers, privileges and immunities of each House and its members and the committees thereof. As far as the constitutional stipulation "until defined by Parliament by law" and the question of defining or codifying the parliamentary privileges are concerned, opinions are divided. It is, however clear that the Constitution makers did envisage codification of privileges by law and Parliament has been avoiding doing so to avoid being subjected to judicial review and scrutiny. The Press and the citizens would naturally like to have greater transparency and to know what precisely are the privileges. For this, earlier these are codified the better.

Imposition of President's Rule

Under article 356, if the President is satisfied that Government of a State cannot be carried on in accordance with the Constitution, he may issue a Proclamation taking over any of the functions and powers of the State Government. The powers of the State Legislature may under the Proclamation become exercisable by or on the authority of Parliament. The State Assembly may be dissolved or kept under suspended animation. The President may take all other steps that may be necessary including suspension of the operation of any constitutional provisions relating to any body or authority in the State except the High Courts. Evey Proclamation must cease to operate at the expiry of two months unless approved by resolutions of the two Houses. After Parliament's approval also, a Proclamation may continue for not more than six months at a time and not for more than a total of three years. But extension beyond one year is not possible even by a resolution of the two Houses of Parliament except during the operation of a proclamation of Emergency and when elections to the Assembly cannot be held (article 356(5)).

Article 356 has been one of the most criticised and controversial provisions of the Constitution. Under this provision, State Governments have been taken over on nearly 100 occasions during the last 47 years *i.e.* on an average more than two States each year. Opposition members and critics have said that the article has been misused, more often than not, for political and partisan purposes by the party in power at the Union level, usually to dismiss State

Governments of parties in opposition. In the Constituent Assembly, while replying to the critics of this provision, Dr. Ambedkar had expressed the hope that it might remain a dead letter and might never be used except as a last resort, after everything else failed. In *State of Rajasthan v. Union of India* (AIR 1977 SC 1361), the Supreme Court held that a Proclamation under 356 depended on the subjective satisfaction of the President and the Court could not substitute its own satisfaction for that of the President nor could it, in view of article 74(2), enquire into the advice given to the President by the Council of Ministers. The Court, however, significantly added that if the satisfaction of the President was *mala fide*, based on extraneous or irrelevant considerations or no satisfaction at all, it could interfere. Thus, exercise of President's power under article 356 was brought under judicial review to that extent.

> ***If instead of serving the people and ensuring provision of justice to all, politicians become merely vote merchants and powerbrokers and remain fully engaged in the struggle for somehow getting to power, remaining there and amassing unlimited wealth for themselves, if scams and scandals follow in quick succession and the houses of our legislatures remain silent spectators or are alleged to have become sanctuaries for the corrupt and criminal politicians and escaadoes from law and if the law-makers and rulers do not perform their assigned tasks, judiciary cannot be blamed for tring to provide in public interest a check and a corrective by asking them to follow the law and the Constitution and to perform their responsibilities of governance.***

In the Bommai case, the Supreme Court stressed the desirability of the question of the majority support of the Government being settled on the floor of the House. This had also been emphasised by the Sarkaria Commission. The latest case in this matter to go before the courts has been that of the "fresh" proclamation of 17 October 1996 "reimposing" President's rule over U.P. The Division Bench of the Allahabad High Court in their judgement of 19 December 1996, even after taking note of the fact that the proclamation had been approved by the two Houses of Parliament, quashed it as *ultra vires* the Constitution.

Much before the judgement came, the present writer had been stressing that since one year of President's rule was completed on October 17, 1996, no proclamation of emergency was in operation and elections had just been held, it was constitutionally impermissible to extend President's rule further without amending the Constitution for the purpose. What even Parliament was barred from doing, could certainly not be done by the Government by giving it a different name of "reimposition" or of "fresh" promulgation of President's rule under Article 356. The Court has upheld this position.

As Justice Lal put it, whatever the subterfuge of a so-called new situation having arisen to justify reimposition of President's rule, the fact was that President's rule was being continued illegally and "thus what cannot be done even by the Parliament (continuance beyond one year) has in effect been done by His Excellency Hon'ble the President of India in the form of a fresh Proclamation....For no fraction of time there was a break. The State of Uttar Pradesh continues to be under President's rule with effect from 18.10.1995 till date without any break....In substance and effect, it is continuation of earlier Proclamation....Impugned Proclamation was not capable of being considered by the Parliament because even the Parliament could not have passed a resolution in the absence of two conditions enumerated in clause (5) of Art. 356....in form there may be two separate Proclamations but in substance it was continuation of the President Rule beyond one year which is expressly barred and prohibited under clause (5) of Art. 356 itself."

Secondly, the present writer had expressed the view that since the Constitution provides that there "shall" be a Council of Ministers, under articles 163 and 164, it was the Governor's constitutional obligation to constitute a popular Government after the completion of the electoral process and the Government so appointed would have been responsible to the Assembly and not to the Governor. If the Governor found it difficult to decide on whom to call to form the Government, he could take recourse to article 175(2), send a message to the House to elect its leader who could then be appointed by him as the Chief Minister. This has also been the very categorical pronouncement of their Lordships of the Allahabad High Court.

Justice Lal says that the term 'Government' used in article 356(1) "refers to elected Government and, not the President's rule". Clause (1) of Article 163 uses the word 'shall'. "The word 'shall' indicates mandatory sense. Therefore, it is not the discretion of the Governor to appoint a Chief Minister or not to appoint. Constitutionally he is bound to appoint a Chief Minister. Here his discretion is limited to choose the Chief Minister if no party has clear majority. But it is not open for the Governor to say that he will not appoint a Chief Minister....political justice can only be extended at this juncture to the electorate through their representatives by adhering to the provisions of Art. 174 & 175 of the Constitution." His lordship bemoaned how the great patriotic people of Uttar Pradesh had been "unconstitutionally deprived of their right of forming a democratic Government." He saw no reason why the Governor could not invoke articles 174 and 175 and ask the members of the Legislative Assembly to indicate the name of the leader in whom they had confidence so that the same person could be appointed Chief Minister.

Justice Kumar forcefully asserted the view that there was nothing wrong in the Governor asking the elected members to choose on the floor of the House a person to lead them as the Chief Minister. In fact, he said, this would be most democratic and constitutional.

> ***Nature does not permit a vacuum. What has come to be called hyper activism of the judiciary draws its stregnth, relevance and legitimacy from the inactivity, incomeptence, disregard of law and Constitution, criminal negligence, corruption, greed for power and money, utter indiscipline and lack of character and integrity among the leaders, ministers and administrators. Should judiciary have no role in polity in the context of open sale and purchase of legislators and sharing of loot of the public exchequer by political mafia gangs?***

The third judge on the Bench, Justice Katju also observed that "it is settled law that a constitutional authority cannot do indirectly what it is not permitted to do directly". His Lordship goes a step further when he holds that in the prevailing situation in U.P., the Legislative Assembly not only can meet but has to meet to decide in whom it has confidence. He adds: "the Governor did have an option, that is, to summon the House under Article 174 and to send a message to it under Article 175(2) informing the House that he was uable to find someone who, in his opinion, was likely to have the confidence of the House, and therefore the House itself should inform him about the person in whom it has confidence. On receiving information from the House, he should have appointed such a person. The matter is now before the Supreme Court.

Political Corruption and Crime

All this apart, the most topical controversies in the field of Legislature-Judiciary interface concern the role of judiciary in matters brought before the courts by way of public interest litigation etc. alleging corruption and other criminal activities indulged in by Members of Parliament and of State Legislatures (including Prime Minister, Union Cabinet Ministers, Chief Minister, Ministers in States etc.)

Strong voices have been raised from the parliamentary fora against the judiciary exceeding its jurisdictional limits and indulging in populism, playing to the gallery and hyper activism. Presiding Officers, Ministers and Members have spoken against the judiciary and not always with the restraint necessary under constitutional culture. Institutional and legal remedies being seriously suggested to combat 'judicial excesses' are taking the following forms:

(i) Since under articles 105 and 194 of the Constitution, members of Parliament and of State Legislatures cannot be proceeded against in courts of law for anything said or vote cast in a House or Committee of the legislature, it is argued that where bribe is alleged to have been given or taken by members in connection with voting on the floor of the House, it is covered by parliamentary privilege and immunity under articles 105 and 194. It is forgotten that there is no immunity in case of criminal offences and giving or accepting of bribe cannot be considered by any stretch of imagination to be "anything said or any vote given".

(ii) Under articles 122 and 212 courts cannot inquire into proceedings of the houses of Union and State Legislatures. A point is, therefore, made that matters connected with the proceedings of a house including matters like voting on the floor of the house cannot be brought before a court. However, it is difficult to comprehend how an act of bribing can be considered to be part of the proceedings of the House.

(iii) As for laws, almost the only provisions in regard to corruption among public servants are in the Indian Penal Code (Sections 161-165) and the Prevention of Corruption Act. The Indian Penal Code which is inherited from the hoary past of the colonial regime, while defining public servants does not specify Ministers or Members among them. The Commission of Public Enquiries Act 1952 refers to matters of public importance but, again, does not specifically mention ministers or members. So far as the Ministers are concerned, it has since been held by the courts that they hold public office. The law by now is pretty well settled that they are covered by the terms like 'public service' or 'public servants'. In Tamilnadu, the Publicmen (Criminal Misconduct) Act 1973 specifically defines publicmen as including the Chief Minister, Ministers and Members of the State Legislature. Several of the State Lokayukt Acts similarly extend to persons occupying offices in public life.

However, whether members of Parliament and State Legislatures are public servants for purposes of the Prevention of Corruption Act has so far not been settled by the Supreme Court. The two High Courts which had occasion to pronounce on the matter differ. While the Bombay High Court has ruled that MPs and MLAs are not public servants, the Orissa High Court has said that they are.

The politician friends would like that the Prevention of Corruption Act is modified to clearly provide that members are not "public servants" and therefore cannot be proceeded against on charges of corruption. Also, they would like that as in the case of senior Government officers, no investigation should be initiated against members without prior permission from the Prime Minister/Chief Minister. In the present climate, it seems to be like saying that a member of the group should not be subjected to any inquiry without prior permission of the leader of the group.

(iv) Quite interestingly, the proposed Lokpal Bill 1996 uses the term 'public functionary' and specifically includes present or past Prime Minister, other ministers and members of Parliament. Also, it covers cases of corruption as defined in the Prevention of Corruption Act, 1988. If the intentions of the proposed law are honest, whatever its defects otherwise, it should settle the question of legislators being public servants for purposes of the Prevention of Corruption Act. But, the way the latest Lokpal Bill is drafted is sinister. Its purpose does not seem to be redressal of public grievances or to combat corruption but to provide protection to politicians against the judiciary everyday unearthing new scandals, scams and skeletons. Once a matter is referred to the proposed Lokpal, all inquiry by the Police, CBI etc. would cease forthwith and any mention in the media would be severely punished.

Separate legislation is proposed to curb 'profligacy' of Public Interest Litigation by imposing requirements like a deposit of Rs. one lakh and restricting the eligibility to apply to those below the poverty line.

'Judicial Activism'

Among the noble aims and objectives of the Constitution, the

Preamble accords the highest place to Justice. All the organs of the State are enjoined to secure to all citizens "Justice - social, economic and political". Even the juxtaposition of words is well conceived and important. If instead of serving the people and ensuring provision of justice to all, politicians become merely vote merchants and powerbrokers and remain fully engaged in the struggle for somehow getting to power, remaining there and amassing unlimited wealth for themselves, if scams and scandals follow in quick succession and the houses of our legislatures remain silent spectators or are alleged to have become sanctuaries for the corrupt and criminal politicians and escapadoes from law and if the law-makers and rulers do not perform their assigned tasks, judiciary cannot be blamed for trying to provide in public interest a check and a corrective by asking them to follow the law and the Constitution and to perform their responsibilities of governance. Nature does not permit a vacuum. What has come to be called hyper activism of the judiciary draws its strength, relevance and legitimacy from the inactivity, incompetence, disregard of law and Constitution, criminal negligence, corruption, greed for power and money, utter indiscipline and lack of character and integrity among the leaders, ministers and administrators. Should judiciary have no role in polity in the context of open sale and purchase of legislators and sharing of loot of the public exchequer by political mafia gangs?

Certain eventualities may be conceived where the judiciary may have to overstep its normal jurisdiction and intervene in areas otherwise in the realm of the legislature: (i) when the legislature fails to discharge its responsibilities; (ii) in case of a hung legislature when the Government it throws up is weak, insecure and busy only in the struggle for self-survival and therefore unable to take any decision which displeases any caste, community or other group; (iii) those in power may be afraid of taking honest hard decisions for fear of losing power and for that reason may have political issues referred to courts as issues of law in order to mark time and delay decisions or to pass on the odium of strong decision making to the courts; (iv) where the legislature and the executive fail to protect the basic rights of the citizens like the right to live a decent life in healthy surroundings or to provide an honest, efficient and just system of laws and administration; (v) where the courts of law are misused by a strong authoritarian parliamentary party government for ulterior motives as was sought to be done during the emergency aberration; (vi) lastly, sometimes the courts may themselves knowingly or unknowingly, become victims of human, all too human weaknesses of craze for populism, publicity, playing to the media and hogging the headlines. After all, as Milton said, fame is the last infirmity of a noble soul. Also, the Courts may try to expand their areas of jurisdiction and arrogate to themselves more functions and powers than legitimately belong to them. It may be said that where an individual or an institution finds conditions congenial to expanding its powers and jurisdiction, it will almost certainly do so.

It is, however, purile to talk of dangers of judicial dictatorship and the like. For, in the ultimate analysis, judgements of the courts have also to be implemented/ and given effect to only by the administration which functions under the political executive. Judiciary has, in fact to be very cautious to ensure that a situation is not reached where its directives are no more fully respected or obeyed. For, if that happens, the last bastion of democracy will also stand demolished and people will lose whatever remains of their faith in the polity.

Judiciary, like the legislature, is also manned by human beings who come from the same social milieu and are subject to same human frailities and social constraints. No institution has monopoly rights to weaknesses or to making mistakes. Courts may also go wrong, overstep the limits of judicial discretion and restraint and make mistakes. Even the Supreme Court recognizes that it is not infallible.

Judiciary, like the legislature, is also manned by human beings who come from the same social milieu and are subject to same human frailities and social constraints. No institution has monopoly rights to weaknesses or to making mistakes. Courts may also go wrong, overstep the limits of judicial discretion and restraint and make mistakes. Even the Supreme Court recognizes that it is not infallible and therefore there have been so many instances of revising and changing its views in the matter of interpretations of laws and the provisions of the Constitution.

In any case, the so-called judicial activism can only provide temporary remedies, It cannot be a permanent solution. Judiciary cannot be a substitute for the legislature. The basic principle to be remembered is that in a democracy, all organs of the State - Executive, Legislature and Judiciary - are responsible and accountable to the people at large. Ultimately, the legislatures and legislators shall have to perform their assigned responsibilities. What has come to be called 'judicial activism' has very wide support and sanction of the people. And, so long as the people are supportive of it, it has all the need and the legitimacy to continue.

PART TWO
LOKPAL

10

THE LOKPAL SCHEME

Inadequate and Incomplete

U.C. Agarwal

Tackling the problem of high level political corruption in India has been a matter of study, debate and discussions for the last many years. No satisfactory and credible arrangements have however been evolved and installed as yet to effectively prevent, detect, investigate corruption cases and launch criminal prosecutions against accused persons. As a result, many holders of high offices like that of ministers in the States or at the Centre seem to have got the impression that they were unanswerable to any outside authority for any of their acts of omission and commission. Some of them, as revealed from the hearing of a few Public Interest Litigation (PIL) petitions before the Supreme Court and the various high courts, recently exercised their self acquired discretionary powers in most blatantly unclean and arbitrary manner lacking basic proprieties and legalities. The illustrative cases are the petrol pump, gas agency, and house allotment matters by two former central ministers. There were of course hosts of other such cases of favouritism and nepotism.

In the petrol pump allotment case the apex court found that Capt. Satish Sharma, the former Petroleum Minister had allotted several petrol pumps and gas agencies to the sons of other ministers, to some of his staff members, to some chairmen of the Oil Selection Boards or their relations and to several other categories of undeserving persons in violation of the laid down guide lines for such allotments. The apex court opined that Capt. Satish Sharma had doled out the petrol pumps as if "he was a king and the pumps were his personal property." The allotment orders were found to be "wholly arbitrary and unconstitutional" and were cancelled by the court, "exemplary damages" of Rs. 50 lakhs were imposed on Capt. Satish Sharma and the CBI was also directed to register a case of criminal breach of trust against him.

In the houses and shops allotment case, the Supreme Court found that Sheila Kaul, the former Housing and Urban Development Minister had allotted 52 shops and stalls to her grandsons and close friends at the prime locations in New Delhi in 1995. These allotments were held to be "arbitrary, malafide and unconstitutional" and were cancelled and "exemplary damages" of Rs. 60 lakhs were imposed on Mrs. Sheila Kaul.

There seems to be an unending flood of scams and corruption cases involving named and unnamed former Prime Ministers, Cabinet ministers and also some MPs. Large scale political corruption has undoubtedly tarnished the image of India and its parliamentary democracy. India is now considered to be one of the top ten most corrupt countries of the world.

Many other mega scams and scandals involving ministers and other politicians that are under CBI investigation or prosecution under the orders of the Supreme Court or the high courts clearly show that cases of abuses of power for personal gains by the ministers in the States and at the Centre have become common and wide-spread. These have caused huge financial losses to the public exchequer and have also aggravated the problem of corruption at other levels of administration. Some of the mega scams do bring to light the menacing dimensions that the unchecked political corruption has reached. These cases include the Bofors scam, the Bank Securities scam, the Telecom scam, the Bihar Fodder scam, the Jharkhand Mukti Morcha (JMM) MP's bribery case, the Jain Hawala case etc. to cite only a few examples. For to list them all would need many pages of space. More and more new scams are getting discovered and reported in the press at frequent intervals. There seems to be an unending flood of scams and corruption cases involving named and unnamed former Prime Ministers, Cabinet ministers and also some MPs. Large scale political corruption has undoubtedly tarnished the image of India and its parliamentary democracy. India is now considered to be one of the top ten most corrupt countries of the world.

The early signs of political corruption were voiced by Dr. S.Radhakrishnan in his speech on the mid-night hour of 14-15 August, 1947 following the famous "tryst with destiny" speech of Pandit Jawaharlal Nehru on the eve of independence in the Constituent Assembly. Dr. Radhakrishnan said, "unless we destroy corruption in high places, root out every trace of nepotism, love of power, profiteering and black marketing which have spoiled the good name of this great country in recent times, we will not be able to raise the standards of efficiency in administration as well as in the production and distribution of the necessary goods of life." How true his warning has proved. This is because no concrete steps were taken to deal with the problem of emerging high level corruption. Before independence, the Prevention of Corruption Act had been passed in March, 1947 and the Delhi Special Police Establishment (or the CBI) had been put on a permanent footing by passing the Delhi Special Police Establishment Act 1946. However, the anti-corruption law and the CBI were generally kept occupied in dealing with lower level corruption cases. The higher political persons, generally, remained outside their purview. Being subordinate to the executive authority of government the CBI was nearly aways afraid to initiate any action *suo motu* against any high level politician or minister even when one of them was reportedly involved in corrupt activities. They were considered to be immune from legal action being themselves the law-makers.

The Santhanam Committee, set up in 1962 to study the rising tide of corruption and to suggest practical measures to deal with the same, stated in its report of 1963: "We hear from all sides that corruption has in recent years spread even to those levels of administration from which it was conspicuously absent in the past." It also sorrwfully reported "we wish we could confidently and without reservation assert that at the political level, ministers, legislators, party officials were free from this malady." Since the country had many great leaders of high moral character and ability at the time of independence, it was hoped that the government of free India would achieve a standard of integrity second to none in the world. The Santhanam Committee however reported "it has to be frankly admitted that this hope has not been realised in full measure."

The committee recommended that specific allegations of corruption on the part of a minister at the Centre or a State should be promptly investigated by an agency whose findings will command respect. For this purpose, the committee suggested that the President of India should constitute a "National Panel" of eminent persons; that an *adhoc* committee of three persons out of the National Panel may be selected on each occasion when a complaint of corruption against any minister is required to be inquired into to ascertain whether there is a *prima-facie* case. The committee had also suggested that as a matter of convention if a complaint is made in writing by 10 or more MPs/MLAs it should be immediately referred to the National Panel for further action. Not much serious thought was given to the above recommendations and the climate of integrity continued to deteriorate.

It was doubtful if the 11th Lok Sabha would last its full term to enact this Bill into law. Most probably like other previous Lokpal Bills this too may lapse.

Later, the Administrative Reforms Commission (ARC) headed by Morarji Desai in its Interim Report of 1966 recommended to set up the institution of Lokpal on the general pattern of the Ombudsman plan of the Scandinavian Countries like Sweden and some Common Wealth countries like New Zealand to probe into complaints of high level corruption. The Swedish Constitution of 1809 had provided for a unique institution know as "Ombudsman" to act as a watch dog on behalf of the citizens to protect them from acts of administrative injustice or abuses of power by any public official—civil, military as also judicial. The word "Ombud" refers to a person who acts as a spokesman or the representative of another person.

Though appointed by the Parliament and hence known as "Parliamentary Ombudsman" the Swedish Ombudsman is independent of all the three wings of the state *i.e.* the legislature, the executive and the judiciary. As a constitutional authority, he enjoys powers under the law to "supervise the observance of laws and other statutes by those exercising pubic activity and that they in all respects properly fulfill their obligations."

The Swedish Ombudsman is neither a super-administrator, nor a super-judge. He however keeps a watch as a constitutional supervisory official over all other public officials including judges so that they function objectively, impartially and in accordance with law. This additional device of check and supervision over all public officials was considered necessary and wholesome in addition to the system of checks and balances through separation of powers between the judiciary, the executive and the legislature. Independent day-to-day supervision was considered necessary to prevent arbitrariness and abuses of power by the holders of public offices.

The Swedish Ombudsman can act on the basis of a complaint or *suo motu*. He has the power to prosecute any erring official including a judge of the Supreme Court. The judicial proceedings against any official proceeded against have, however to be conducted in the normal judicial courts. The Ombudsman himself cannot inflict any punishment. He only sets the law into motion where even required.

Many other countries have adopted this Swedish institution of Ombudsman according to their own social, administrative and political systems and traditions. For example, New Zealand the first Commonwealth country to have adopted the system in 1962 excluded courts of law from the purview of their Ombudsman (known as Parliamentary Commissioner) to preserve their long tradition of judicial independence—an independent judiciary to guard against the excesses of the executive. Only the executive officials including ministers came under the Ombudsman's jurisdiction in New Zealand.

The Lokpal should have its own investigating and prosecuting agencies. Under the present Lokpal Bill, the Lokpal is empowered only to utilise the services of the state investigating agencies like CBI with the "concurrence" of government.

The ARC in India in its Report (1966) on the subject stated: "Our study of the institution of Ombudsman in Scandinavian countries and the Parliamentary Commissioner in New Zealand and the working of these functionaries convinces us that we can suitably adopt these institutions for our needs. These institutions are generally, a supplement to the Parliamentary control independent of any political affiliation, outside the normal administrative hierarchy, and free from the formalism, publicity and delays associated with governmental machinery."

The final recommendations of the ARC provided for two separate authorities designated as "Lokpal" and "Lokayukta". The Lokpal was meant to deal with complaints against ministers and secretaries to government and the Lokayukta with complaints against other public officials. The judiciary was kept outside their purview as in New Zealand. These institutions were basically meant to deal with public "grievances" relating to acts of mal-administration and "allegations" involving corruption. The Bills on the subject introduced in 1968 and 1971 in Parliament were therefore called "The Lokpal and Lokayukta

Bill 1968/1971". These however lapsed without becoming law. During the Janata regime of Morarji Desai in 1977 there was some rethinking on the scope of this legislation. It was decided that to begin with only the institution of "Lokpal" be set up at the Centre to deal with allegations of corruption against "Public men" as there was no institution to deal with political corruption.

The idea of a separate institution of "Lokayukta" at the Centre was deferred as already the Central Vigilance Commission had been set up on the recommendations of the Santhanam Committee to deal with corruption complaints against "public servants" or officials. Similarly there were other departmental and semi-judicial machineries to deal with public "grievances" not involving corruption. The 1977 Bill was accordingly named as "The Lokpal Bill 1977". No reference to "Lokayukta" was made in this Bill. The Lokpal under this Bill was to deal with complaints of "misconduct" against "public men". The definition of "public men" included only central ministers, members of Parliament and the State Chief Ministers. "Public servants" or officials of any category, were not included. The definition of "misconduct" mainly related to abuses of power by any public man for personal gain including any undue gain or favour to his relatives or associates.

This Bill too however lapsed after the fall of the Janata government in 1980. The 1985 Lokpal Bill introduced during Rajiv Gandhi regime excluded the Prime Minister, the State Chief Ministers and the MPs from the jurisdiction of the Lokpal. However, even this truncated legislation was not enacted. The 1989 Lokpal Bill introduced by the V.P. Singh government made little change in the earlier Bill of 1985 except to bring back the Prime Minister within the Lokpal's purview. This Bill too was allowed to lapse. The latest Lokpal Bill of 1996 introduced by the Deve Gowda government has brought back the MPs in addition to all central ministers including the Prime Minister within the purview of the Lokpal. The Lokpal, under this Bill, is to deal with offences punishable under the Prevention of Corruption Act 1988. It was doubtful if the 11th Lok Sabha would last its full term to enact this Bill into law. Most probably like other previous Lokpal Bills this too may lapse. The following are however some of the basic defects and deficiencies of the Lokpal scheme as incorporated in the 1996 Lokpal Bill as also in the earlier Bills.

First, under section 11 of the Lokpal Bill 1996 the Lokpal can act only on the basis of a complaint and not *suo-motu*. In fact under

Section 33(b) of this Bill the Lokpal has been prohibited to make any inquiry "upon its own knowledge or information". Generally, Ombudsman in most countries (barring UK) have the power to act *suo-motu.* For example, the Ombudsman in Denmark, like his other Schandinavian counterparts is required under the Law to keep himself informed as to whether any person under his jurisdiction pursues unlawful ends, makes arbitrary or unreasonable decisions or otherwise commits mistakes or acts of negligence in the discharge of his duties." The Ombudsman is not to wait for a complaint to act against any erring official or public man. Had a Lokpal with such powers been in position in India he could have, on his own, taken action against arbitrary allotment of petrol pumps, gas agencies and government residential houses and shops to undeserving persons by the ministers concerned. Host of other such abuses of power could have been stopped by a properly empowered Lokpal by issuing warning notes to concerned officials or ministers. In fact, the existence of a Lokpal of this type would have been by itself a preventive check. In the World Ombudsman Conference held in New York in 1986, which the author attended as an official delegate from India he was told by some other Ombudsmen that they do telephone or write to public officials if any wrong doing comes to their notice and their warnings nearly always prove effective to nip the mischief in the bud.

Secondly, the Lokpal should have its own investigating and prosecuting agencies. Under the present Lokpal Bill, the Lokpal is empowered only to utilise the services of the state investigating agencies like CBI with the "concurrence" of government. The CBI investigations of the various scam cases like the Jain Hawala case, the Bihar Fodder scam case, the JMM bribery case etc. have shown that but for the intervention and monitoring of these cases by the Supreme Court and the High Courts these would have made little progress. The prestige and powers of the apex court and the high courts and the public admonitions of the CBI by them alone could make the agency work over time to expedite investigations. Even so there are lingering doubts if these investigations would be thorough and unbiased. It is all the more doubtful if the Lokpal with his limited powers over the CBI, a government agency, could be as effective to chase it to investigate cases entrusted to it speedily, objectively and impartially. The CBI personnel, barring some exceptions, are more likely to safeguard their own future interests by suitably obliging politically well placed persons if they have to investigate cases against any one of them. Some of them may consider discretion to be better part of valour. More desirable arrangement would be to allow the Lokpal to have its own separate investigating and prosecuting agencies and permit him only additionally to make use of government agencies if required. That would make the investigations speedy and more credible.

> ***CBI personnel, barring some exceptions, are more likely to safeguard their own future interests by suitably obliging politically well placed persons if they have to investigate cases against any one of them. Some of them may consider discretion to be better part of valour.***

Thirdly, under section 24(2) of the Lokpal Bill 1996, a complainant is liable to punishment of imprisonment for a term "not less than one year and which may extend to three years" besides fine upto Rs. 50,000 if he fails to prove the allegations made in the complaint. It would have been too much to have expected from private complainants to prove the type of high level corruption charges that were investigated recently by the CBI under court orders. For example, could a private party prove the allegations of corruption in the Hawala cases, the Fodder scam, the JMM bribery case etc. Through PIL petitions, the burden of investigations was rightly placed on the CBI and the courts started monitoring the progress of investigations. The courts have also drawn upon the healthy concept of "*amicus curiae*" (friends of the court) to utilise the services of some eminent legal luminaries to assist them in marshalling of evidence and in looking into breaches of the law in the important scam cases. The PIL petitioners have not been left to their own resources to prove the allegations. If the Lokpal leaves such matters to any individual complainant to prove, he would hardly serve any useful purpose in tackling the problem of high level corruption. In fact, the fear of punishment and the burden of proving the allegations by the complainant may discourage any one to approach the Lokpal with such complaints. The Lokpal may thus turn out to be a protector of the corrupt rather than be a people's watch-dog to ensure probity among ministers.

Fourthly, Lokpal Bill 1996 provides that the inquiry of the Lokpal has to be in camera and any premature publicity of this is punishable u/s 23(3) by the Lokpal. The punishment may extend to six months imprisonment and fine up to Rs. 10,000. Since there is no limit to the duration of inquiry, it is likely that a wrong doer may get undue protection from adverse publicity. Secret inquiries also do not inspire public confidence. Normally the inquiry should be open unless in any particular case the Lokpal decides otherwise.

Fifthly, even after a complaint is proved to be *prima-facie* true, the Lokpal can only send his findings to the appropriate "competent authority" for necessary action u/s 17(1)(b) of the Bill. The Prime Minister is the competent authority for all other ministers and the Lok Sabha for the Prime Minister. Thus while the Lokpal can himself punish a complainant if his complaint is found to be false, he can also punish any one who prematurely publishes the inquiry, he can do no more than make recommendations to the competent authority regarding the action to be taken against an accused even when he is found to be at fault. The Lokpal has no power to launch any criminal prosecution against any accused even after the complaint is found to have *prima-facie* evidence of truth. The Lokpal can do little if the competent authority does not comply with his recommendations. He can only report this to the Parliament.

The Lokpal scheme was first visualised in the sixties. In the meanwhile there has been rapid deterioration in the values, and standards of political culture and behaviour. Criminal elements with money and muscle powers weild immense powers in the affairs of political parties. A good number of them also hold offices of power in the central and State government and abuse these for personal gain and enjoyment. The Lokpal scheme of 1968 vintage is totally inadequate for the present day requirements. By delaying action on the Lokpal legislation for over two decades, the problem of corruption has now become acute, and wide spread as revealed by the hundreds of mega scams. The suspects are no longer a few junior ministers but are a large number of senior ministers at the Centre and in the States including some former Chief Ministers and even Prime Ministers. The old Lokpal scheme would no longer be an effective remedy to deal with this aggravated problem. The age old saying that a stitch in time saves nine had unfortunately been ignored so far. Now therefore more radical measures are called for. This has also been demonstrated by the apex court and the High Courts by their handling of the PIL petitions. The present phase of "judicial activism" has clearly brought out the need to install a Lokpal who could fulfill the role of the higher judiciary to check maladministration and corruption in high places. For this purpose the Lokpal needs to be given appropriate legal powers.

To make the Lokpal institution really effective and meaningful it should be made a constitutional body like the C&AG, the Election Commission and the higher judiciary. That would give the institution greater dignity, prestige and status befitting his functions of dealing with complaints against ministers. The major defects pointed out earlier need also to be removed. The Lokpal should have the power to act on his own, and have its separate investigating and prosecuting agencies. The Lokpal need not depend on the decision of the "competent authority" for launching prosecution but should have powers to make such decisions himself.

The fear of punishment and the burden of proving the allegations by the complainant may discourage any one to approach the Lokpal with such complaints. The Lokpal may thus turn out to be a protector of the corrupt rather than be a people's watch-dog to ensure probity among ministers.

The present Lokpal scheme has rightly been found to be faulty by many critics for being inadequate and out of date. A low profile Lokpal-a crusador without a sword—is unlikely to reduce the workload of the apex court and the High Courts who have been of late handling corruption complaints through PIL. The aggrieved parties would continue to knock their doors through PIL petitions rather than approach a fake and powerless Lokpal.

11

DEMOCRACY, CORRUPTION AND LOKPAL BILL

Bindeshwar Pathak

Against human greed, no system is immune
Aristotle

When Edward Gibbon (1737-94) was asked to tell in one word the cause of the fall of the Roman Empire, the British historian was a stunned man. The monumental book which took 25 years to write was, quite understandably, hard to compress in one word. Gibbon became tense for a moment and said in typical British undertone: "Corruption, Yes corruption, amorality and lust for power and sex destroyed the Roman Empire which ruled almost the entire known world for more than 300 years, ruthlessly and without compunction." It would have been quite pathetic to see the last Roman emperor Diocletian captured and caged by vandals, Huns and barbarians, paraded in Constantinople and speared to death, bringing to an inglorious end (in 476 BC) an empire, the like of which was never seen in the history of mankind.

The single most dangerous source of decay of a system is corruption which destroys the moral fabric of a society and faith of the people in their leaders. Corruption skews planning, and development process; it destroys the credibility of institutions, slows down growth, and eats into the vitals of democracy. Take any country in Latin America, Asia and Africa, and we will find that corruption has almost destroyed the credibility of the system. The Benazir government had been sacked for corruption and India is slowly heading for a major political crisis in the system, following chargesheeting of leaders of major parties for venality. Political leaders are lining up before jail, leaving political fixers and satraps to run the system. According to reports about Rs. 400 crore in FERA violation, Rs. 133 crore in urea scam, and Rs. 750 crore in fodder scam are lost. It is estimated that Rs. 50,000 crore, which is six times last year's total deficit in the Union Budget, is lost in bribe during the past five years in a poor country like India where children are dying of hunger, and women have no adequate clothes to hide their womanhood, nor is there enough medicine in hospitals to save the bread-winners of poor families. Italian style scams and scandals have shaken the Indian system. Legislators from nearly all political parties have flouted basic norms of public behaviour. They obey no rules, follow no principles, display no sense of public responsibility. What Gibbon said was true of the Roman empire, and truer of India.

Yet another dangerous effect of growing corruption is the loosening of national cohesiveness. It is true that in the US, the States (13 in the beginning) created the Centre (federation) while in India, the Centre created States whose boundaries have been made and re-made periodically. And, the centrality of the Indian Union has created a strong sense of national unity among diversities. But, this argument cannot be taken too far. India is essentially a country divided against itself and held together more by force than persuasion. There are many Bosnias in India which is sharply divided along linguistic, (18 major languages) social and cultural identities and groups. In fact, the Indian civilisation has been very inclusive, absorbing outside influences. But the result of this historical process of assimilation has been widening and deepening fault-lines in our society which in times of a weak central government begin to pose a threat to its unity. Diasporas from Bangladesh, Nepal and Tibet have become threats to many States in the North-East where major agitations against aliens produced a revolution in Assam that shook the entire country. The Gorkhaland agitation in West Bengal, Bangladeshi stir in Tripura and Assam and Tibetan presence in Himachal. Sir Winston Churchill said in 1931; "India is a geographical term, no more a united nation than the Equator."

We gave to ourselves democracy right from the day one without creating basic conditions for democracy to take root. Education among them being most important; only educated and literate people can make right choices. That being not there, we have the people in legislature, many of whom should have been in jail. It took Britain, for instance, more than 300 years since Robert Walpole (1676-1745), the first British Prime Minister, for democracy to grow in stages through Magna Carta (1215) Petition of Rights (1628) *Habeas Corpus* Act (1670), the Bill of Rights (1689) etc. In the US, democracy, which is more a mindset than a system, came along with immigrants, who were scientists, scholars, adventurers, persecuted and convicts, but all were educated. George Washington finally settled the unity issue in the battlefield while Thomas Jefferson condified it in the American Constitution, the briefest and most original ever written in any country.

Democracy is a complex system which only educated people can operate and make it deliver goods. Plutarch has said that Greece, which had such a glorious past, with its wealth, its empire, its prestige, collapsed through one single malady-its "uncontrollable freedom and the licence of its assemblies. Whenever those ignorant men met in the theatre—inexperienced and untrained in every aspect—they committed themselves to useless wars; they put trouble-makers in charge of the state and turned out of the city those who had served it well." Other Greek philosophers also said that, democracy produced mediocracy and incompetence, as a result of which the Greek empire fell to become a vassal state of Rome supplying soldiers, teachers and mistresses to Roman rulers.

However, democracy continued to fascinate man, specially after World War-II when colonies started becoming free one after another with democratic systems in place. The long-left hunger to be self-governing drove the "poor, illiterate and untrained" people of Asia, Africa and Latin America to give to themselves rights which they could not exercise with responsibilities. No wonder Africa, more than any other continent, became a land of unstable political regimes. In a continent of more than 500 million people and 51 countries, military coups and violence transferred power from one influential group to another, much more frequently than in any other continent. Between 1960 and 1982, there were 56 coups and 102 attempted coups in the sub-Saharan region alone. In Burundi, more than a million people were slaughtered recently in a conflict between two tribes, Hutus and Tutsis. Nigeria, Rwanda, Liberia, Somalia and many other countries are high on carnage lists. Most countries of Africa, made free from European powers, (French, British and Dutch), were trying to operate the democratic system and ended up in killing each other because democracy has been alien to Africa's ethnic cultures. These countries are facing hunger and death.

Former colonial powers, in the name of democracy, plundered these countries of their raw materials, including gold, diamond, timber, hide and skin and so forth and provided arms to ethnic groups who indulged in carnage. These powers fuelled civil war in Angola and toppled the government in Zaire in 1965. In 1977 and 1978, Washington and Paris airlifted troops and materials to crush uprising in Shaba (Zaire) only to take the country deeper into economic crisis and political instability. However, there had been multi-party elections almost in all African countries and all of them failed.

The threat to democracy in India is from corruption, illiteracy and poverty (people with *zero tomorrow*, as Dostoevsky says), demographic expansion, caste, language and regional divisions and from the Constitution itself which has prescribed a parliamentary system that promotes, and does not prevent, divisive tendencies. The greatest of all threats is from corrupt politicians who have shaken the foundation of Indian Republic, quite forgetting that they cannot enjoy their ill-gotten wealth if society is destroyed. Adams had said: "Democracy never lasts long; it soon wastes, exhausts and murders itself. There never was a democracy that did not commit suicide!"

As a matter of fact, if the checks and balances system, as provided in the Constitution, had been working effectively, this bill would not have been necessary at all. The bill is clearly an unwanted intervention in the constitutional process.

The Lokpal Bill has to be studied against this historical background. As a matter of fact, if the checks and balances system, as provided in the Constitution, had been working effectively, this bill would not have been necessary at all. The bill is clearly an unwanted intervention in the constitutional process. But, despite what is wrongly called judicial activism, the institutional framework of the country has failed to stem the tide of corruption as was done in the US when Nixon was forced to step down on what appeared a simple burglary report by the *Washington Post* correspondent, Bob Woodward. The entire American system rose as one to oppose the US President, the most powerful man in the world, and he had to resign in disgrace and died a sad man.

In India, the institutions legitimised wrong doing in many cases either by overlooking the politician-criminal nexus or by legitimising it. The mismatch between the growth of Indian democracy, largest in the world, and the strength of institutions to protect and promote it has resulted in corruption and the bad governance of the country. Various options, or a combination of options have been considered these past decades during which corruption grew to become a threat to the system. The *Lok Ayukta* and *Upa Lok Ayukta* have been working in some States, including Maharashtra, for many years. They are empowered to inquire into complaints against government officers and Ministers. In some States the jurisdiction has been extended to include the Chief Ministers.

The Ombudsman concept was first mooted in Sweden in 1809. Over the years, this grew to become an institution to hear the grievances of the people, a work which has been done in different countries by different institutions like Parliament Commissioners in Britain, the Mediator in France, *Ianobayan* in the Philippines and *Wakaque Mohtased* in Pakistan. Lok Adalats in India are also an extension of this concept.

The negative features of the Bill far outweigh the positive ones. The Chairman and the two members are to be appointed by the government. The committee thus not only consists of the very persons that the Lokpal is supposed to investigate, but also is clearly controlled by the government and is hardly likely to proceed boldly against powerful politicians. There is also total lack of transparency; for, the Lokpal proceeding will be held in camera. It will also be a punishable offence for anyone who will report the proceedings.

No fewer than five attempts have been made (1968, 1971, 1977, 1985 and 1990) to have a Lokpal law adopted by Parliament. But, it did not happen; either Parliament was dissolved or the bill just lapsed without anybody noticing it. Now, the Lokpal Bill, in its amended form, was introduced in Parliament on September 13, 1996. This Bill is also bogged down in controversy over a variety of contradictions. The Lokpal Bill proposed to cover the Prime Minister and members of Parliament, present and past ministers, and inquire into complaints against them. Under Lokpal regime the MPs and ministers will have to periodically disclose their assets which otherwise they are supposed to be doing under income-tax laws. The basic assumption of the Bill is that persons in high places should be accountable to the people and there would be an independent machinery to investigate charges against them.

The negative features of the Bill far outweigh the positive ones. The Chairman and the two members are to be appointed by the government. The only other requirement is consultation with a committee of seven persons—the PM, the Speaker of Lok Sabha, the Home Minister, the Personnel Minister, the Vice-President and the leaders of Opposition of both Houses of Parliament. The committee thus not only consists of the very persons that the Lokpal is supposed to investigate, but also is clearly controlled by the government and is hardly likely to proceed boldly against powerful politicians. There is also total lack of transparency; for, the Lokpal proceeding will be held in camera. It will also be a punishable offence for anyone who will report the proceedings. While the Lokpal is examining a complaint, they have the power to stop normal criminal investigations into offences by such persons. And, if the complaint is found false (even if it is not frivolous), the complainant is liable to be sent to jail or fined up to Rs. 50,000. These provisions will prevent the exposure of wrong doing by the Press. Under the Bill, the Lokpal can neither prosecute the person nor recommend his prosecution. He can only send his report to the "competent authority". Even if "competent authority" decides to take action, which they are not compelled to do, it would probably mean registering an FIR and setting the wheels of the normal criminal justice machinery into motion. The Lokpal Bill will thus, frustrate judicial activism which holds people in high offices accountable to the people. It will also hurt the regime of the public interest litigation which has done a lot of good to the system and the people.

We may continue to read into the prints of the Lokpal Bill and suggest any number of amendments, but it will not change the corruption situation in India which is too deep-rooted to be cured by superficial, inadequate and a half-way measure like this ill-fated Bill. Corruption is also a problem of malfunctioning of the system and collapse of institutions which work together in a pre-determined manner to produce a wholesome polity. To be true, politics has become big business of our times. People join politics and spend fortune to become office-holders not to serve the people or do the job well and retire to their professions after a time, but to misappropriate public money. This is the fact that we should not pretend to be not knowing.

This Bill should be scrapped which apart from other shortcomings, violates the basic principle of Indian constitutionalism. This will simply become yet another cover for politicians to do evil things and get away under its cover. Having done that, the leaders of the country should summon courage and re-write the Constitution, switching over to the presidential system with the following redeeming features, among many others.

> ***To be true, politics has become big business of our times. People join politics and spend fortune to become office-holders not to serve the people or do the job well and retire to their professions after a time, but to misappropriate public money. This is the fact that we should not pretend to be not knowing.***
>
> ***This Bill should be scrapped which apart from other shortcomings, violates the basic principle of Indian constitutionalism. This will simply become yet another cover for politicians to do evil things and get away under its cover. Having done that, the leaders of the country should summon courage and re-write the Constitution.***

The President, on the American pattern, will be both head of the state and government. He can be the President only for two terms of five years each. The financial and executive powers should be balanced between Parliament and President. If deadlocks arise, they may be solved as is done in the US where there are only two parties, representing the broad spectrum of economic and political preferences of the people, unlike in India which is a fractured society based on caste, creeds, economic and regional disparities, far too wide apart to be reconciled or represented by two parties alone. The terms of the members of Parliament should also be limited to two and no one found guilty in any criminal offence *prime facie* by the first court should be allowed to contest election or vote. Now, the situation is that until a man is finally found guilty in a lengthy legal battle which may last lifetime, he or she can continue to fight elections and hold office. Once the *prima facie* principle is established, the criminals will be stopped in the track to legislature. By way of systemic reforms, it is also necessary to make education compulsory so that only literate people could vote. There has to be a time-bound programme for full literacy (and family planning) in the country which alone can strengthen institutions, the ultimate safeguard of democracy.

This may be a tall order but there is no other way to abolish corruption and make the system work. And, it is a must to save the people and the country.

12

COMMENTS ON THE LOK PAL BILL

J. Veera Raghawan

There are a few issues to be highlighted. First, there is the question about the appointment of the Lokpal. There is a view that when the Prime Minister is empowered to take very vital decisions affecting the entire country, he should also be trusted to take decisions regarding the appointment of the Lokpal. It is recognised that there is currently considerable mistrust about appointments being credible. Howeverr, this point of view stresses the importance of keeping a distinction between the office of the Prime Minister and the person of the Prime Minister. An individual may fall short in some respects, but that does not mean that the office of the Prime Minister has to be denigrated. In accordance with this view, it would be rather inappropriate to deny to the government the right to take decisions regarding the appointment of the Lokpal and to tie it down to the recoomendations of a Committee. Opposed to this, there is the view-point that as the Lokpal will look into the complaints about the ministers including the Prime Minister, he should not be appointed by the government or even on the recommendation of a Committee presided over by the Prime Minister. He should rather be appointed through the binding recommendations of independent body of eminent persons.

The credibility of the institution of Lokpal is of utmost importance in the prevailing atmosphere of distrust of constitutional authorities.

It is best to provide for appointment through a committee of independent persons and make the entire appointment procedure as transparent as possible. The clause relating to the procedure for appointment of the Lokpal, therefore, needs to be amended accordingly.

The second important aspect to be considered is that: Will the Lokpal be provided with adequate staff and facilities? It would not be right to hamper the Lokpal by requiring him to get approval of the government in regard to his Secretariat. It is, therefore, not correct to provide that he will have such staff as the government may determine in consultation with him from time to time. Such a provision exists in respect of the Comptroller and Auditor General and by and large it has not worked very well. In fact, Dr. Ambedkar while debating this specific clause in the Constituent Assembly, had expressed his misgivings in this matter. His misgivings have proved valid and there is need for empowering the Lokpal to determine his own staff. In the absence of such empowerment, safely "charging" the expenditure to the Consolidated Fund of India, will not ensure the requisite independence.

Further, it is wrong to provide in the Bill that the government can transmit any complaint to the Lokpal and he shall be bound to investigate such complaints. It is for the Lokpal to decide what work is of imprtance and how much he can do within his resources and what priorities he should give. Otherwise, it is possible to flood the Lokpal with much of an important work thus preventing him from discharging the responsibilities in regard to the main items. In fact, the Comptroller and Auditor General Act provides that before government can issue any order entrusting any work on C&AG they should consult the Auditor General. In practice, it is the hope that the Auditor-General would advise the entrustment of only such work to him which he considers essential and that such advice would be honoured. The clause for entrusting additional work from time to time by government should either be deleted or in the alternative, it should be provided that such work can be entrusted to the Lokpal only with the prior consent of and on the conditions stipulated by the Lokpal.

Another aspect refers to access to documents. There should be complete and free access to all documents for the Lokpal to successfully carry out his work. During the emergency, restrictions were placed on the Auditor-General in regard to access to documents on the ground that Audit was concerned only with implementation of policy and not with policy formulation. But it is at the stage of policy formulation the intentions become clear and the manipulations become obvious.

Finally, there is really no basis for holding the hearings in camera and to shut out all press publicity. Once a *prima facie* case is established, all discussions should be open. The Lokpal Bill should not become a convenient way of concealing from the public misdeeds of those in authority.

All these years, there have been agitations by many for having a Lokpal Bill but when one is ready and is on the anvil, it is not correct to oppose the Bill on account of difference of opinion on certain clauses. The broad thrust for the Lokpal Bill is one which is acceptable to all the political parties and it is hoped that the Bill will be enacted soon with modifications.

13

LOKPAL BILL, 1996

Missing Ombudsman

S.S. Singh

The Lokpal Bill, 1996 is sixth in the series on the subject. The first Bill titled 'Lokpal and Lokayuktas' was introduced in May 1968 which was referred to the Joint Select Committee of both Houses of Parliament. JSC submitted its report in March 1969. In August 1969, the Bill was passed by the Lok Sabha. The Bill lapsed due to the dissolution of the House in July 1970. A Bill with certain modification was again introduced in August, 1971 but this also lapsed. A Lokpal Bill was again introduced in the Lok Sabha by the Janata Government in July 1977. Once more it was referred to JSC and again lapsed due to the dissolution of the House. The Congress Government in August, 1985 introduced another Bill which was once again referred to the JSC. This time the Government withdrew the Lokpal Bill without advancing convincing reasons. The National Front Governemnt in 1989, yet again introduced the Lokpal Bill which again lapsed due to the defeat of the Government on the floor of the Lok Sabha while seeking the vote of confidence.

So far the institution of Lokpal at the national level is the victim of dissolutions, defeat and deferment resulting in conceptual confusion and adversely affecting the establishment as well as the existing Lokayuktas in States. The approach of the political parties have already delayed the establishment of Lokpal institution by more than 30 years. How long the citizens of this country will wait for this institution is not yet certain. It would not be out of place to remark at this stage that in successive Bills the idea and ideals of the institution of Lokpal (ombudsman) have undergone a great metamorphosis.

So far the institution of Lokpal at the national level is the victim of dissolutions, defeat and deferment resulting in conceptual confusion and adversely affecting the establishment as well as the existing Lokayuktas in States. How long the citizens of this country will wait for this institution is not yet certain.

Ombudsman Jurisprudence

The Ombudsman institutions have been considered the dominent accountability mechanisms of the second half of the century. There is now widespread acceptance that parliamentary politics alone are inadequate to the task of calling the modern executive to account. Executive power has increased, is increasing and has to be checked. The Ombudsman institution is considered to be a symbol of the democratic government, facilitator of development and protector of citizens. The Ombudsman according to Caiden, is "an institutionalised public conscience - the essence of what governments ought to do; that is to cultivate the well being of the citizen; the preservation of the individual liberty and the equitable treatment of all citizens by the public bureaucracy." It is a flexible friend of public administration. There is also some evidence that the ombudsman office has been "aggrandised...beyond just a citizen's defender or protector into a citizen's advocate, thereby crossing the administrative realm of government into more publicly controversial ground."

The hallmark characteristics of the classical ombudsman are independence, impartiality, access to information, power to investigate and opportunity to report to the legislature as opposed to the executive arm of government. There must be no public interest defence against an ombudsman investigation. The office of ombudsman should be user friendly and accessible. The task of the ombudsman is to see to the best of his ability that all who hold authority and power retain a sense of responsibility towards the individual citizens. Citizens in a democratic society should not feel that they are under the governance of the rule of man. The role of the ombudsman is to establish and promote the governance of the rule of law.

Former Australian Commonwealth Ombudsman, Dennis Pearce,

wrote in his Final Report, 1990, that the objectives of the ombudsman are to improve the quality of administration and to provide a mechanism for individuals to obtain redress by:

a) identifying instances of defective administration through independent investigations;

b) encouraging agencies to provide remedies for members of the public affected by defective administration;

c) identifing legislative, policy and procedural deficiencies, and encouraging systemic improvements to overcome those deficiencies; and

d) contributing to advice to the government on the adequacy, effectiveness and efficiency of the various means of review of administrative action.

For India, Ombudsman (Lokpal) means greater accountability of administration and better access for the common man to grievance resolution. It should be seen as a part of the total drive for the de-professionalisation of the legal process and de-feudalisation of the administrative culture. Addressing corruption *expost facto*, without first attending to the business of reforming and improving administration is like putting the cart before the horse. Therefore, addressing public grievances, both through the operation of the ombudsman system and through improved internal procedures, would have a direct impact on the level of corruption existing at any given moment.

Lokpal and Administrative Reforms Commission

The ARC in 1966 was requested to consider, *inter alia*, the problem of redress of citizens' grievances, keeping in view the need for ensuring the highest standards of efficiency and integrity in the public services, and also for making public administration responsive and responsible to the people. The ARC was expected to examine the following:

- the adequacy of existing arrangements for redress of grievances; and

- the need for the introduction of any new machinery or special institution for redress of grievances.

The ARC in its interim report, recommended that statutory machinery should be established to investigate complaints alleging corruption or injustice arising out of maladministration. The point which needs to be emphasised in this context is that the ARC recommended the creation of new machinery in the form of Lokpal to tackle both an "allegation" as well as "grievances" and not to inquire the allegations of political corruption only.

Lokpal Bill 1996

The latest Lokpal Bill was introduced on 13 September, 1996 for the establishment of Lokpal to inquire into allegations of corruption against public functionaries" which was referred to the Parliamentary Standing Committee on Home Affairs by the Speaker of the Lok Sabha. The provisions of the Bill need to be closely and carefully examined in the light of the evolving ombudsman jurisprudence and core values of this institution. From statement of objects and reasons of the Bill one can clearly have an impression that the Bill provides for setting up the office of Lokpal to give effect to the recommendation of the ARC. However, the hope created would be demolished if one proceeds to the details of the Bill. In this way one may perhaps like to call this Bill as deceptive, proposing an institution to deal with political corruption and claiming to give effect to the recommendation of the ARC.

From statement of objects and reasons of the Bill one can clearly have an impression that the Bill provides for setting up the office of Lokpal to give effect to the recommendation of the ARC. However, the hope created would be demolished if one proceeds to the details of the Bill. In this way one may perhaps like to call this Bill as deceptive, proposing an institution to deal with political corruption and claiming to give effect to the recommendation of the ARC.

Appointment

For appointment of Chairman and Members, a Committee is provided under clause 4(1) to recommend names for consideration of the President. The Prime Minister as Chairman and Minister incharge of the Ministry of Home Affairs and Minister in-charge of the Ministry of Personnel, Public Grievances and Pensions in the Government of India, in our view, should not be associated with the appointment process. It is so because they are within the jurisdiction of the Lokpal institution and also on the requirement of impartiality and fairness. Therefore, a committee may be constituted on the following pattern:

1. Chairman of the Council of States	Chairman
2. Chief Justice of India	Member
3. Speaker of the Lok Sabha	Member
4. Leader of the Opposition in Lok Sabha	Member
5. Leader of the Opposition in the Council of States.	Member

(If there is no leader, a person may be nominated by the opposition members for this purpose).

Under clause 4(2) of the Bill there is a need to mention the requirement of quorum of at least 3 members including Chairman.

Term of Office

Clause 6(1) of the Bill stipulates that every member shall hold office for a term of five years. There is no mention of the maximum age. There is a need to mention the maximum age at 70 or 72 years to save this office from becoming rehabilitation centre for the retired persons. At the time of appointment care should be taken to appoint a person of independence, reputation and integrity. However, it should be remembered that charismatic personalities are not born every minute.

Removal of a Member

Clause 7 of the Bill needs to be redrafted with a view to make the removal of the Chairman and a member in consonance with that of the Chief Justice of India and a Judge of the Supreme Court. The following provision is suggested;

"A member shall not be removed from his office except by an order of the President and on the ground of proved misbehaviour or incapability after an inquiry made by the sitting or retired judge of the Supreme Court in the same manner as for the removal of a Judge under the Judges (Enquiry) Act, 1968. The inquiry report shall be placed before both the Houses of Parliament and each House shall pass an address for removal by a majority of its total membership and a majority of not less than two third of its members present and voting."

Jurisdiction and Procedure of Inquiry

Clause 9(1) should be redrafted. Lokpal should be given power to investigate any action taken by or with the approval of a minister including Prime Minister or a Secretary or any other public servant (Joint-Secretary and above). Such an investigation could be undertaken if a person made a complaint either registering a "grievance" or making an "allegation". The terms "grievance" and "allegations" should be defined in accordance with the provisions under the Lokpal Bill, 1971.

The Lokpal institution should be armed with a core investigating agency, entirely at its own disposal. In this regard Karnataka and Madhya Pradesh Lokayukta models might be adopted. The Lokpal should be given *Suo motu* power of investigation to protect community and collective rights of the depressed, deprived and downtrodden sections of the society. It should also be given power to review and revise its own decisions/recommendations under appropriate circumstances. The Lokpal should be given power to send an interim report pending final investigation. The requirements of an affidavit under clause 11(2) and one thousand rupees fee under clause 11(3) are prohibitive provisions, therefore, they should be deleted.

The proceeding before the Lokpal in a preliminary scrutiny of complaint may be in camera. The regular inquiry by the Lokpal and members should not be held *in camera*. However, the Lokpal should be empowered to decide on the mode of inquiry from case to case. In case it take a decision to inquire in camera than it should provide reasons in writing for doing so. Transparency in the inquiry proceedings before the Lokpal should be adopted as a general rule. Such a procedure will remove suspicion of any kind. Therefore, clause 13(2) should be redrafted. In addition, there should not be any public interest defence in the investigation by the Lokpal. There is no need of clause 15(4).

Declaration of Assets and Liabilities

Every member of Parliament shall furnish a return of all assets owned by him and members of his family and all liabilities incurred by him and the members of his family before Lokpal every year in such form as may be prescribed according to the requirement under clause 18 of the Bill. This clause needs to be redrafted stipulating the powers of Lokpal in case of failure on the part of the members of Parliament. The term "family" needs to be explained in terms of who constitute the family.

Miscellaneous

The clauses under this part of the Bill need to be reconsidered in the light of suggestions made above. Care should be taken to facilitate the person(s) who are willing to come forward and help the system to improve. They should be facilitated rather than prohibited. However, there is no need of clause 26 and that should be deleted. This clause gives wrong signal to the people.

Concluding Remarks

The above discussion on the Lokpal Bill, 1996 reveals that the Bill in the present form is not an attempt to establish Lokpal (Ombudsman) institution. At the best, the Bill can only be called as Permanent Commission on Political Corruption. To give effect to the ARC recommendation we have to bring both "allegation" and "grievances" within the jurisdiction of Lokpal. It should also be remembered that the Lokpal institution is not the panacea for all the ills prevailing in the system. For efficiency and effectiveness of the Lokpal institution it is essential that adequate internal methods of redress in the form of complaint machinery need to be established. There is a strong and urgent need for proper attention on the total system for handling grievances within the Government of India. Finally, it should be remembered that in a society where corruption and maladministration are systemic, horizontal accountability to outside authority like Lokpal institution and other, *viz.* auditors, judiciary etc, requires the vertical support of civic society. Civic monitoring groups can set up hotlines, support whistle blowers, develop associations of the users of governemnt services and mobilise different interest groups of the people and the press. Anti-corruption and accountability reforms will remain dead letters unless officials are determined to implement them.

14

LOKPAL

Need for Ombudsmanic Culture in India

R.D. Sharma

The emergence of the institution of Ombudsman in governmental sector was due to the fact that there was increasing awareness of and public disquiet over the ability and competence of the existing institutions of government to handle and respond to complaints about their activities in a fair and reasonable manner.

Ombudsman is an institutional device for grievance-resolution and one of the methods for securing administration justice. The citizens are entitled to complain against specific acts of their rulers and that their complaints need to be investigated by an institution completely independent of the executive.

In Sweden, the Chancellor of Justice was introduced by King Charles XII in 1713. Even before 1713, way back in 13th century, in Sweden as well as in Finland, there were officers who may be considered as predecessors of the Chancellor of Justice. Originally styled as Supreme Prosecutor, the officer was to exercise a general supervision "to ensure that laws and regulations were complied with and the public servants discharged their duties properly."

In the Venetian Republic, there was the famous Lion's Mouth into which the people were invited to place their grievances and complaints against government. During Mughal ruler Jhangir's reign, there was the famous "Bell of Justice" which could be rung by any grieved citizen who was to lodge a complaint against government servants including the King himself.

The Danish Parliament had enacted a constitutional law in June 1953, for providing the institution of "Ombudsmand" (Danes uses "d" instead of "n") as a Parliamentary Commissioner to supervise the civil and military administration of the state. Ombudsman is a Swedish word meaning "a representative or agent of the people or a group of people, an officer appointed by the legislature to handle complaints of administrative and judicial action".

In United Kingdom in 1932, the Committee On Minister's Powers- Donoughmore Committee was required to report on delegated legislation and administrative justice. This committee had suggested the constitution of a Committee for scrutinising administrative rule-making and giving reasons for administrative decisions.

The Franks Committee was thus, constituted to recommend only on administrative justice. The Committee recommended the creation of a Council of Tribunals with advisory powers to keep the functioning of administration under review.

In 1957, a Committee headed by Sir John Whyatt, submitted a report to "Justice" - the United Kingdom's section of International Commission of Jurists entitled: "Citizens and the Administration - The Redress of Grievances". In its report, this Committee set down an answer to the inquiry into the adequacy of the existing means for investigating complaints against administrative acts or decisions of the government departments and other public bodies where there was no tribunal or statutory procedure available for dealing with such complaints.

In India, for the first time after independence, it was an academic duo - Professor Karve and Bodh Raj Sharma who, in 1950 had suggested the institution of Ombudsman for India. Soon after, in 1951, A.D. Gorewala, in his report on Public Administration had mentioned certain machinery for the improvement of the "integrity or moral standards of, as well as efficiency in the administration". He had recommended a tribunal of enquiry for ministers and for high government officials for purposes of finding out facts but without powers to take any action. This tribunal was to be appointed by the President for the central government.

Later in 1957, Dr. C.D. Deshmukh, in his Srinivas Shastri Endowment Lecture at Madras University had suggested a high level impartial Standing Judicial Tribunal.

Despite forceful recommendation and appeal by the Administrative Reforms Commission in special interim report on "Problems of Redress of Citizen's Grievances", in 1966, the government of India remained cool towards creation of an office of Ombudsman for India, although such an institution was created in two cities of Israel namely Tel-Aviv and Jerusalem (1966) and also State Commissioner and Comptroller of Complaints for Israel, in 1966.

So far as the developing countries are concerned, in Guyana, Director of Public Prosecutions in 1965 and in Mauritius in May 1966 an Ombudsman - like officer was appointed. In U.K. the Parliamentary Commissioner for Administration (PCA) was for the first time appointed in 1967. In the same year three new plans were initiated to appoint PCAs for Alberta, New Brunswick and Hawaii. Very recently in New Zealand, the office of Ombudsman was installed countrary to the point of view that countries with administrative courts may not find favour with such an institution. Professor Rowat, a world renowed researcher in the field of administrative justice has vehemently refuted the logic that "administrative law courts do no need Ombudsman like institution."

In Sweden, at the moment, there are three Guardians of the Law *viz,* Chancellor of Justice - an official of the Crown, Parliamentary Ombudsman - for civil affairs and Ombudsman for military affairs.

In Zambia, an African country, there is an Ombudsman-like institution called Investigator - General with three Commissioner subordinates who directly report to the President of Zambia. Thus, it is a multi-member institution.

Earlier to the Zambian experience, Tanzania, way back in 1966, had appointed a Permanent Commission of Inquiry - a Tanzanian version of the institution of Ombudsman. The Zambian Ombudsman was created in 1973 called Commission for Investigations. Another African country, Nigeria, has a Chief Complaints Commissioner at federal level and State Complaint Commissioners as Ombudsmen for the States or federal units.

In Britain, at present, there is a Parliamentary Commission for Administration, not exactly as Swedish Ombudsman but as an adjunct of Parliament and also a Commissioner for Local Administration as well as a Health Service Commissioner. In U.K. there is another officier called Police Complaints Authority. In one word, there is a whole system of regulatory bodies which operate to hear, *inter-alia,* complaints against the newly provided utilities under the Acts. There is a very extensive list of bodies who perform Ombudsman like functions. At present there are seven Ombudsmen working U.K.

Principle Enshrined

It is universally acknowledged that the machinery for dealing with complaints against discretionary and arbitrary decisions should embody the principle of *impartial adjudication* which should be achieved by providing to the aggrieved persons, with a right to appeal to an independent authority, unless otherwise there exist over-riding considerations which make it necessary, in the public interest, for the final decision to be left to the independent, impartial, chief executive of the State-the President or the King as the case may be.

Appointment

The Parliamentary Commissioner Act of 1967, in U.K. created the office of the Parliamentary Ombudsman to be appointed by the Crown, removable by an address from both the houses of Parliament for incapacity on medical grounds.

In Scandinavian countries, the Ombudsman is appointed by Parliament to investigate the complaints from citizens against unfair administrative action. Ombudsman is, thus, a Parliamentary institution to protect citizens against arbitrary authority.

In India the first bill on Lokpal was introduced in Parliament in 1968 *i.e.* two years after the publication of Administrative Reforms Commission's special interim report on "Problems of Redress of Citizen's Grievances". In the original bill, all the powers of Ombudsman were provided but in later versions of 1971, 1977, 1985 and 1989 there were attempts to compromise with the concept, powers and jurisdiction of the institution which rendered the entire attempt redundant. The basic malady behind is the fear of the executive of the Ombudsman.

Powers, Areas and Jurisdiction

Ombudsman is described as "institutionalised public conscience". It is in essence of what government ought to do "to cultivate the well-being of the citizens, preservation of individual liberty and the equitable treatment of all citizens by public bureaucracy."

The primary task of an Ombudsman is to see, to the best of his ability that all who hold authority retain a sense of responsibility. Sir Oliver Franks had once said that "an aggrieved individual can always complain to the appropriate authority, to the members of Parliament, to a representative organisation or to the press..."

The powers of Ombudsman are derived from the statutes relating to the mode of appointment, protection of tenure, right to decide cases, right and access to information, *suo-moto* and the procedure of removal. It is also the right of Ombudsman to report to the Legislature.

In U.K., the Parliamentary Commissioner for Administration is approached by any aggrieved citizen with a written complaint, who has sustained injustice in consequence of mal-administration. In the first instance such a complaint must be made to an M.P. within 12 months of the person aggrieved first having notice of matters alleged in the complaint.

It is the primary responsibility of a democratic government to provide satisfactory instrument for the speedier redressal of grievances of the citizens. The institution of Ombudsman is an attempt to pacify quest of citizens for impartial investigation of arbitrary actions of public servants. The hallmark characteristics of Ombudsman are independence of action from executive, impartiality coupled with unimpeded action, unhindered inquiry, uninterrupted access to information and undeterred courage to report "truth" to the legislature.

The institution of Ombudsman should be user-friendly or citizen-friendly, inexpensive and accessible. In India, the appointment of Lokpal will be an attempt to provide transparency in the functioning of much-maligned and criticised politico-administrative system. It will help to re-furbish and re-introduce its lost credibility, responsiveness and fairness in all the fields of governmental functioning.

Lessons for India

Members of Parliament who would be required, hopefully soon enough, to debate the Lokpal Bill now pending in Lok Sabha should bear in mind the following considerations.

1. *Constitutional Status For Lokpal*

The institution of Lokpal needs to be given constitutional status with the amendment of the basic statute, in order to check powerful influence of the executive and to make the institution, in real sense, independent of it. It will also ensure permanency, continuity, superiority and fearlessness. A Lokpal thus be appointed after each general election, as it is the practice in U.K.

2. *Multiple-Membership of the Institution of Lokpal*

It is only proper that the Lokpal is conceived as a multi-member institution so that the gravest danger of single individual becoming authoritarian could be avoided. The appointment of Lokpals should be made by the President of India after consulting the Speaker of Lok Sabha, Chairman of Rajya Sabha and the Chief Justice of India, from amongst sitting or retired judges of the Supreme Court. The President of India need not be bound by the advice of Prime Minister in the appointment of Lokpals.

Removal

Lokpals could be removed on the ground of misbehaviour or incapacity after an inquiry by a retired or a sitting judge of Supreme Court in the same manner as it is provided for the removal of a judge under Judges (Enquiry) Act 1968. The inquiry reports should be placed in both the Houses of Parliament by their Chairmen and in case, a resolution is passed in both the houses with 2/3rd majority of the members present and voting, supporting such a resolution, Lokpal would stand removed.

Jurisdiction

The Lokpal should have jurisdiction to investigate and report on both "allegations", as well as "grievances" against public servants or any of the public functionaries except President of India.

Lokpal must also possess *suo motu* power to investigate in order to protect individuals against arbitrariness of governmental functionaries. The institution should also exercise "review power", in order to facilitate revision of its own previous decisions.

The Lokpal should have power to conduct searches and seizures of documents necessary for investigation with the help of its own investigatory unit like RAW. This Core-Investigating Agency (CIA) be placed entirely at the disposal of Lokpal and should have authority to summon the services of existing investigating agencies of the Union or the States.

The Lokpal should have powers to summon any public servant of the government either of the Union or of the State, a board, authority, or any local or municipal, rural authority or private company etc. for deposition or as witness along with any document in his possession. The Lokpal should have power to require attendance of any person for deposition or as witness except the President of India.

Presentation of the Report

The Lokpal should have the "right to report to the Parliament" as and when the President of India so desires about the results of its investigation. It should be duty-bound under the statute to publish every year its report in order to made it a public document after the presentation to the Parliament.

The Cabinet Secretary, the secretaries of each ministry of the Union as well as State governments, the personnel secretaries, the managing directors of public and private companies and corporations should be compulsorily required under statute to be personally liable for non-compliance or non-production of relevant document or record. The Lokpal should have the power "to punish" for non-compliance as its contempt which may be confinement from six months to six years.

Parliamentary Select Committee

It is strongly recommended that the Speaker of Lok Sabha appoint a Parliamentary Select Committee, on Lokpal in order to ensure smooth functioning of this three-member Commission. Such a Select Committee will also ensure its independence. It would also ensure protection of Lokpal from all-powerful executive authority.

15

AMENDING THE LOKPAL BILL

Abdulrahim P. Vijapur

The Constitution of India promises to create a political system which is truly democratic and based on the principles of "equality before law" and "the due process of law". Powers and immunities apart, no citizen can be treated above law and go scot-free by violating it even when he/she happens to be a Prime Minister, Minister or member of Parliament. The recent phenomenon of corruption at high places has brought to fore the necessity for introducing a Lokpal Bill' in Parliament in September 1996. The Bill has many lacuna in it and need to be amended drastically. To make the Bill effective it may need to be amended or a new draft may have to be prepared and reintroduced in the Parliament for its consideration and passage. The following points are suggested for consideration which should guide the drafting of the revised bill:

The bill should seek to set up the office of Lokpal with Chairman and four Members. The Chairman, who has been a Chief Justice or judge of the Supreme Court; two members who have been Chief Justices or judges of high courts and two members who are eminent and acknowledged public persons of impeccable integrity and morality. It should have a fixed tenure. They should not be removed by the executive except through impeachment. The Lokpal should inquire into complaints alleged against public functionaries such as: the past and present Prime Ministers, Union Ministers, members of Parliament, Chairmen of Public Sector Undertakings, higher Civil Servants like Secretaries, Additional Secretaries, Joint Secretaries and Deputy Secretaries of the Union Government, under the Prevention of Corruption Act, 1988, and the Criminal Procedure Code.

The Lokpal should be appointed by the President of India on the recommendations made by a Committee consisting of: (i) The Prime Minister—Chairperson, (ii) A Former Prime Minister, (iii) Leader of Opposition in the Lok Sabha, (iv) Chairman of Rajya Sabha, (v) Chief Justice of India and (vi) Home Minister of India.

The Bill has many lacuna in it and need to be amended drastically. To make the Bill effective it may need to be amended or a new draft may have to be prepared and reintroduced in the Parliament for its consideration and passage.

The Bill should provide that the Lokpal shall inquire, *suo motu* or on a petition presented to it by any person, public servant (as he has inside information about corrupt practices) or an aggrieved person/party. Enquiries should not be conducted only under the Prevention of Corruption Act 1988, they should also be under Cr. P.C. It is well know that the Anti Corruption Act covers only cases of illegal gratification and possession of assets out of proportion to the lawful sources of income. Cases of corruption arising from nepotism such as the grant of agencies of petrol pumps to one's relatives or cases like the one concerning St. Kitts forgery do not directly fall under the purview of Anti Corruption Act. The Lokpal should also have to approach courts on its own to prosecute the guilty.

Lokpal should invariably submit its reports to the Parliament. These documents should be made public. For example, the stipulated rule in the Bill that every member of Parliament shall furnish a return of all assets owned by him and members of his family before the Lokpal every year but the public cannot have access to this information needs to be amended the electorate should have a right to know the assets of their representatives.

Since all persons inquired into are theoretically equal in the eyes of law, its inquiry reports should be submitted only to Parliament, and not to the PM in case of Ministers etc.

The proceedings of Lokpal should be held in public unless it decides to hold them in camera in matters involving national security. If this is followed, based on the proceedings or important disclosures arising from it, public spirited men can initiate PIL. Moreover, if the inquiry is conducted in camera, the complaint may experience harassment, or threats to his life from government machinery. Judicial enquires should normally be open to the public. If the proceedings are held in camera the judicial principle of "equality of arms" is violated.

If these recommendations are agreed upon by the general public and the members of Parliament, a better draft of Lokpal can be approved by the Parliament. These suggestions will go a long way in making Lokpal an effective institution to root out corruption in high places.

16

WILL LOKPAL BILL DO THE JOB?

Surat Singh

Corruption in public places results in loss of credibility of the government. It takes away the clarity of direction and paralyses the political will; so to make democracy successful and to inspire confidence of the people in it, rooting out corruption among public functionaries becomes top priority for any good governance.

The present Lokpal Bill-1996 states in its statement of objects and purposes that the Bill provides setting up the office of Lokpal with Chairman and two members for a fixed tenure. Under the scheme of the Bill, the Lokpal will inquire into complaints alleging against public functionary including the Prime Minister of India an offence punishable under Prevention of Corruption Act-1988. The statement of the objects and purposes of the Bill promises that the Lokpal would be able to act in an independent manner and it will carry out the objects and purposes of the recommendations of the Administrative Reform Commission for enabling citizen to have recourse to convenient and effective forum for determination of complaints and thereby save him from pursuing his remedy through process of courts which may prove expensive or dilatory. These are the promises of the Bill. We have to inquire whether the Bill would be able to do the job.

To be an effective institution, two basic elements are to be satisfied. First that the institution has sufficient capacity to perform its assigned task. Second that the Institution has sufficient will to perform the task assigned to it. Thus both willingness and capacity to do the job are needed. Now, if we analyse the Lokpal institution as proposed to be set up under the Bill, certain important features will emerge:

That there will be a Lokpal consisting of one Chairman and two members. The Chairman will be equivalent to the Chief Justice of India and two members would be the persons who are eligible to be appointed judges of Supreme Court. But these appointments will be made by the Committee as per section 4 of the Act. The Committee will be headed by the Prime Minister of India having a Speaker of the House and Deputy Chairman of the Council of States, Minister in charge of the Ministry of Home Affairs in the government of India, Minister in charge of the Ministry of Personnel, Public Grievances & Pension in the government of India, leader of the Opposition in the House of People's and leader of the Opposition in the Council of States as members of the Committee.

> ***An important factor in making institution of Lokpal effective would be as to how quickly and effectively the Lokpal would be able to decide the complaints placed before it. As per the present scheme of the Bill of 1996, it is laudable that section 13 of the Bill provides a time limit of maximum one year to complete the inquiry.***

From the above provisions, it is quite clear that the appointment of the Lokpal and two other members will be made by the executive head-Prime Minister of India who himself may be an accused in the proceedings before Lokpal because the it may inquire into allegations of public corruption against Prime Minister also. If the experience of last 5 years of India is to be taken into account, even former Prime Minister of India Narasimha Rao was not beyond repproach. In fact, if the allegations of CBI in JMM Bribery Case is to be believed then even former Prime Minister did not hesitate to bribe several MPs to buy their votes to retain his seat. Under such circumstances, appointment of the Lokpal by a Committee which is headed by Prime Minister will not inspire such confidence. The better proposal would be that let a committee of five seniormost judges of the Supreme Court headed by Chief Justice of India should make the recommendations for the appointments of the Chairman and the members of Lokpal.

Another important factor in making institution of Lokpal effective would be as to how quickly and effectively the Lokpal would be able to decide the complaints placed before it. As per the present scheme of the Bill of 1996, it is laudable that section 13 of the Bill provides a time limit of maximum one year to complete the inquiry. But the serious lacuna in the Bill is that once the Lokpal it as completed its inquiry, Lokpal is not authorised to take the action on its own report like Supreme Court. But it has to submit its report in writing to the competent authority and the competent authority shall examine the report forwarded to it within 3 months from the date of receipt and will decide about the action taken or proposed to be taken on the basis of the report.

As per section 2-b **'competent authority'** under the Bill has been defined in the following manner. The 'competent authority' in relation to the Prime Minister of India means House of People, and in case of member of Council of Ministers, the Prime Minister of India, in case of member of Council of States, the Council of States and the House of People's in case of member of that House.

It is respectfully submitted that if the Prime Minister would have been able to take action against corrupt Ministers or the House of People's has been able to take action against a corrupt member, there was no need for judicial intervention as we noticed these days. So the submission of the Lokpal report to competent authority for appropriate action will only delay and dilute the action to taken against a delinquent public functionary. In this connection, it is recommended that like Indian Supreme Court, the Lokpal should be able to take the action on its report itself without any reference to anybody.

Another point which deserves attention is that though the Chairman of the Lokpal and members of the Lokpal have been given the status cf Chief Justice of India and judges of the Supreme Court respectively under the Bill but the procedure for their removal has not been kept the same as is applicable to Chief Justice of india and judges of the Supreme Court. As per the Indian Constitution, the Supreme Court judges can only be removed by impeachment but in case of Lokpal under section 7 of the Bill, the member can be removed by an order made by the President on the ground of proved misbehaviour or incapacity after an inquiry made by the Chief Justice of India in which the member had been informed of the charges against him and given reasonable opportunity of being heard in respect of those charges.

If Chairman of Lokpal and members of the Lokpal are given the status of Chief Justice of India and judge of the Supreme Court respectively, the procedure for their removal should not be diluted from the one laid down in the Constitution for removal of the Supreme Court judges by impeachment, otherwise the Bill is likely to be declared unconstitutional.

Indian Supreme Court has been able to inspire the confidence of the people by exposing corruption in public because of its independence and its statesman-like vision of preserving the basic values of the society, without fear or favour. In fact, talking about American Supreme Court famous American Professor Alexander Bickel in his book, on American Supreme Court entitled *'The Least Dangerous Branch'* has pointed out that the task of Supreme Court is to preserve the basic values of society because the politicians might not be able to take tough and unpopular decisions because they have to get re-elected. But since Supreme Court judges have the security of their tenure and they are chosen from trained professionals, they can reflect upon larger issues of the society. Likewise, the institution of Lokpal can help us in maintaining our basic values and reflect upon larger issues of morality in public places if the institution of Lokpal is properly constituted and sincerely implemented. But the present Lokpal Bill - 1996 is far from satisfactory and suffers from several flaws as indicated above. So unless the above mentioned flaws are removed, it is good to continue with the present system of Special Courts dealing with cases under the Prevention of Corruption Act and the Supreme Court having supervisory power over them, than this highly flawed proposed Lokpal Bill.

17
LOKPAL AND DEMOCRACY

Suresh Kulkarni

Social change is generated by floating ideas about the proposed change, by crystallising the proposed ideas into a Bill and by ossifying the Bill into an Act. This is one approach followed in India's democratic governance. The approach, however, does not ensure that wishes of the people are incorporated in legislative actions.

This does not mean that the legitimacy of legislative measures must be questioned. What is being implied is that success of the measures will depend on people's consent. This can be accomplished by putting intended actions of the state to public debate.

Against this backdrop, the Lok Pal Bill now on the anvil appears to suffer from serious defects in some major respects:

(1) The Bill like many other legislative and social measures is a transplant of the British model of 'citizen participation in administration'. It was first reommended in 1966 by the Administraive Reforms Commission. It is being repiloted now and even forms part of the Common Minimum Programme. But the Bill departs from the British model in one crucial respect. The model kept trials of cases against ministers and public functionaries untouched by the Ombudsman. The Indian Bill specifically empowers the Lokpal to stay any pending proceedings in a criminal case if a complaint is filed.

(2) The most dreaded parts of the Bill relate to: (a) its provision for proceedings being conducted under secrecy (Section 13(2)) and (b) its provisions for treating reporting by outsiders on its proceedings or revealing the identity of complainant a cognizable offence (Section

30(1) C and (3)). These sections clearly take away from citizens even the existing rights to lodge complaints or move the court to issue directions against erring functionaries.

(3) The powers conferred on the Lok pal to conduct the proceedings in secrecy implies that it will keep the complaint in constant fear of being proved guilty or wrong unilaterally or arbitrarily. Thus the very act of complaining is nipped in the bud. Could the Bill be clearer on its intentions of disregarding citizens' legal rights?

(4) Section 26 is another disturbing element in the Bill. In case the Lokpal does not find a complaint sustainable or tenable, no prosecution shall lie and no court can take cognizance of the offence or "substantially the same allegations in the complaint".

> ***The present Bill appears to give blanket protection to Ministers and other public functionaries against acts of omission and commission. If the functionaries' fears of being prosecuted for their wrongs are removed then citizens might as well bid bye to democracy.***

Legal luminaries have many skeptical observations to make on the Bill. The spirit of the Lokpal institution should be that of transparency and promotion of participatory democracy. This does not belittle the importance of the rulers but will only create caution in their minds that they are being watched for stray acts if any. The present Bill appears to give blanket protection to Ministers and other public functionaries against acts of omission and commission. If the functionaries' fears of being prosecuted for their wrongs are removed then citizens might as well bid bye to democracy.

18

OMBUDSMAN

Grievance Man or Allegation Man

Mohinder Singh

In the past 30 years there has been an extraordinary spread of ombudsman systems across the globe. Some label it "ombudsmania". Ombudsmen now operate in over forty countries, both developed and developing.

Interestingly, the office of the Ombudsman has emerged distinctly different in developing countries *vis-a-vis* the developed ones. Countries such as Norway, Denmark, New Zealand, Australia, Canada or UK are adhering to the original Swedish model of the "grievance" man. But developing ones such as all the 9 African countries with the Ombudsman or all our 12 States of India with the provision for *Lokayukta* perceive it essentially as an instrument of investigating allegations of corruption or misconduct by ministers and other public officials.

Admittedly, there can be element of overlap between the two functions. Yet developed countries are basically using the office of the Ombudsman for providing relief to people from administrative failures and injustices. Not that they are free from corrupt practices but they use other agencies—quite elaborate and effective at that—for the purpose. Developing countries also have specific agencies for investigating corruption such as our CBI or Anti-corruption departments or Vigilance Commissions or ultimately courts and a Commission for Human Rights, too. Yet curbing corruption stays such a high-profile concern that the office of the Ombudsman has been grasped as another agency towards that end.

The Lokayukta Acts of Rajasthan, Andhra Pradesh, Madhya Pradesh and Himachal Pradesh have incorporated only "allegations", omitting "grievances". Indeed in some States, former Vigilance Commissions have been converted into office of the Lokayukta. In UP, a complainant has to use a prescribed form, accompanied by an affidavit and a fee of Rs 1,000.

Lokayukta Acts in few States do not rule out grievances but the thrust is almost entirely on investigating allegations of corruption or misconduct. Sometimes an idea is mooted that the Lokayukta can have two separate wings, one attending to allegations, the other to grievances. But the same has not evoked any serious response. The selection of Lokayukta and the work procedures are geared to investigating corruption, not lapses in administration.

Similarly all the thinking over the Lokpal (it has yet to become law despite nearly 30 years of legislative activity) is centred on combating corruption in ministers and top officials. And such high hopes have been built upon it that the actual Lokpal may come as a let down.

This overriding emphasis on attending to allegations instead of grievances has one important outcome. Dealing with allegations commonly calls for a judicial process. You need judges for it, not eminent men experienced in administration and public life. Anyway higher judiciary evokes the kind of public trust that top bureaucrats and other professionals no longer enjoy in the country. No wonder our ombudsmen are all retired justices, whearas in developed countries they are mostly persons with an administrative background.

In a way the classical Ombudsman has an easier time. The disadvantage of handling corruption cases arises from the fact that most of the subjects of investigation are highly articulate and educated, possessing considerable manipulative skills. These they use to spread lies and misinformation, let alone delaying and obstructive tactics.

The classical model of Ombudsman has been fairly successful in making the administration more humane. Not only he helps a substantial number of individual cases, he plays a significant role in improving administrative procedures and norms. He is easy to access and quick to respond.

The methods employed are investigatory, not adversorial. With his patent impartiality and understanding approach, the Ombudsman often enjoys commendable cooperation from government agencies. And though he only makes recommendations, these are almost always complied with. Anyway a time limit is usually prescribed for compliance. In case a government agency is unwilling to comply, it must have this decision taken at its highest level.

The system has its critics. For instance, right-conscious, educated individuals are overrepresented in complaints while the disadvantaged are underrepresented. And there are delays in disposal of cases; the average time in UK to deal with a grievance is one year.

A question naturally arises. Can this model be successfully transplanted into developing countries? Problems arise when the rules prove harsh in particular cases. In everyday administration, cases of blatant delay, deliberate vexation or outright favouritism are rather rare.

In the prevailing conditions, merely putting in a grievance machinery wouldn't be enough Unfortunately the grievance machinery is mostly used by government servants to ventilate their problems, and little utilised by the general public. The situation calls for manifold administrative reforms: streamlining systems, simplifying procedures, reducing controls and permissions, fixing responsibility of various officials. A classical ombudsman, besides being a person of stature and manifest integrity, should preferably be knowledgeable about the sector entrusted to him.

It is made out that the classical ombudsman functions best when an administration has reached at this stage. Our priorities are yet different. First we have to remove endemic corruption and favouritism, irregularities and misconduct.

What is the relevance of rules when you simply can't obtain a "completion certificate" for your house or a "fitness certificate" for your bus without paying a bribe? More radical changes, both in administration and societal attitudes, are needed.

Lokayuktas in Maharashtra, Madhya Pradesh and Andhra Pradesh may have had some success but elsewhere the impact of this version of ombudsman has been minimal. In UP, for example, quite a few recommendations for action against errant officials lie ignored. The experience of the African countries hasn't been much better. Even Nigeria, with its elaborate system of Ombudsman at the centre and in regions, has recorded scant success.

In the prevailing conditions, merely putting in a grievance machinery wouldn't be enough. In fact we have quite an elaborate machinery for redressing public grievances at different levels of our administrative system. Directorates of Grievances at Centre and States, and departmental grievance set-ups.

Unfortunately the grievance machinery is mostly used by government servants to ventilate their problems, and little utilised by the general public. Again the machinery is often ineffective. It remains just a conduit, passing on the complaints to the concerned authorities. Lok Adalats and Consumer Courts are doing good work but still their role is limited.

The situation calls for manifold administrative reforms: streamlining systems, simplifying procedures, reducing controls and permissions, fixing responsibility of various officials, and so on. Yet alongwith, the "grievance" ombudsman can be given a fair trial. It's too good an innovation for redressing grievances and improving administrative working to be given up as impracticable in our existing conditions.

Take Delhi. There could be an office of Ombudsman for general city administration, such as law and order, schools, hospitals, roads and so on. This means dealing with the work of State administration, MCD, NDMC, and other local bodies. Another office could be there for public utilities such as DESU, MTNL, DTC, and bodies like DDA. Someday one for the scheduled banks and another for the public sector insurance companies.

A classical ombudsman, besides being a person of stature and manifest integrity, should preferably be knowledgeable about the sector entrusted to him. Unlike Lokayuktas with their quasi-judicial approach, the grievance man should have rich administrative experience. And not necessarily a man long into retirement; he could be younger, more energetic.

In our conditions, it's quite likely that the office of the Ombudsman would be flooded with grievances. It's for him to evolve a suitable system of priorities and operate informal procedures. Crucial to the success of the scheme that the ombudsman's office doesn't get routinised or bureaucratised.

The ombudsman, or whatever name is given to him, can only function well if the cornered government departments and agencies view him as an ally in improving their working, not a threat. Cooperation has to be forthcoming during investigation and his recommendations treated with respect. This actually calls for a certain work culture and sensitivity on the part of top political and official establishment.

Admittedly these conditions are not easy to manage. Yet if the office of the Ombudsman gains the confidence of the public, it will be an important addition to the armoury of responsive governance.

19

THE LOKPAL BILL

Subhash C. Kashyap

The latest Lokpal Bill was introduced in Lok Sabha on 13 September 1996. The Bill, its history, its changing complexion and focus, its present motivation and the proposed provisions need to be examined in depth and discussed widely before the politicians are allowed to get away with it and succeed in their nefarious design to escape all public exposure and judicial scrutiny of their conduct behind the facade and smoke screen of the proposed Lokpal.

The origins of the concept of Lokpal can be traced back to the Scandinavian institution of the Ombudsman. The main function of the Ombudsman in those countries is to deal with public grievances in matters connected with:

(i) Misuse of administrative discretion,
(ii) Maladministration,
(iii) Administrative delays, and
(iv) Administrative corruption.

It may be recalled that the Administrative Reforms Commission in 1966 recommended the setting up of the Lokpal and Lokayukta institutions to deal with political corruption and maladministration somewhat on the pattern of the Scandinavian Ombudsman. Since then, as many as five official attempts have been made to bring about legislation on the subject. Bills were introduced in 1968, 1971, 1977, 1985 and 1989. Some of these were examined also by Joint Parliamentary Committees which went round more than once on 'Bharat Darshan' tours. The 1968 Bill was even passed by Lok Sabha.

This and three others lapsed due to the dissolution of the House while the fifth one was withdrawn by the Government. Those who were closely connected with the progress of these Bills in Parliament and the Government approach thereto were witnesses to the fact that irrespective of the party in power, no Government was really ever sanguine or serious about making any of these legislative proposals into law. They were largely viewed as a recipe for marking time and diverting public attention or as substitutes for action on widespread complaints of corruption and public grievances against maladministration.

Although it is called the Lokpal Bill, its relationship, if any, with the institution of Ombudsman or with the Lokpal proposed by the Administrative Reforms Commission or even the Lokpal as outlined in the earlier aborted Bills on the subject is tenuous and phoney. Infact, the name seems to have been purloined to camouflage its real intentions of protecting the corrupt and misleading the people.

The Bill has nothing to do with public grievances or wrong doing by the state machinery, with misuse of administrative discretion, with maladministration or undue delays, with injustice in individual cases or the like. In fact, it excludes from its direct purview the conduct of civil servants and administrators at any level. It applies only to the present or past Ministers including the Prime Minister and Members of Parliament. Also, it is confined to only cases of corruption as defined in the Prevention of Corruption Act, 1988.

Apart from the fact that from the drafting point of view the Bill makes a sad reading and is full of drafting and printing howlers, it has any number of provisions to which serious objection can be taken on grounds of propriety, principles and public interest. Constraints of space do not allow analysing all these.

The proposed Lokpal has been barred from starting any enquiry on its own. There must be a complaint, fees have to be paid and full responsibility taken by the person making the allegation of corruption. If the complaint is found to be baseless, serious punishment extending to 2 years in jail and 50 thousand rupees in fine will befall the complainant.

While under the 1968 Bill, the Lokpal was to be appointed after consultation with the Chief Justice and Leader of the Opposition in Lok Sabha, the three-member Lokpal now proposed would be appointed on the recommendations of a Committee consisting of 7 persons. With 3 Ministers (including P.M.), Speaker, Dy. Chairman

Rajya Sabha and two leaders of the Opposition. In the absence of a clear provision to the effect that the recommendations would have to be unanimous, it is important to underline that the nominees of the ruling party or Front would always be in a majority on the committee and in case persons not acceptable to the Opposition are appointed on majority recommendations the institution itself may become redundant and dyfunctional.

While the Chairman of Lokpal has to be from among the present or past Chief Justices or judges of the Supreme Court, the two members may also be from among those 'qualified' to be judges of the Supreme Court. If merely such qualification is enough, there would be thousands of advocates - many of them also party politicians - with requisite seniority who would become eligible to be considered.

While the 1968 Bill which was considered by a Joint Parliamentary Committee and was actually passed by Lok Sabha in 1969 clearly envisaged public servants making complaints to the Lokpal and the latter keeping their names secret, the present Bill categorically excludes them from those who can approach the Lokpal [clause 11(1)]. Disclosure - printing or publishing - of any information in respect of any complaint of corruption under this legislation when the inquiry is in progress and until three months after the report has been forwarded by the Lokpal to the Prime Minister or a House of Parliament, as the case may be, has been made punishable (clause 23).

> ***Although it is called the Lokpal Bill, its relationship, if any, with the institution of Ombudsman or with the Lokpal proposed by the Administrative Reforms Commission or even the Lokpal as outlined in the earlier aborted Bills on the subject is tenuous and phoney. Infact, the name seems to have been purloined to camouflage its real intentions of protecting the corrupt and misleading the people***

Clause 14 empowers the Lokpal to give directions for deferring or suspending any ongoing police investigations in matters covered by the complaints made to it.

Jurisdiction of the Lokpal has not been positively defined anywhere. Clause 9(2), in fact, at first gives the clear impression that "Lokpal may inquire into any act or conduct of any person *other than a public functionary*". One has to read special emphasis on the use of the word 'complaint' in the preceding sub-clause (1) and then go back to its definition in clause 2 to find out that the jurisdiction of Lokpal actually extends to public functionaries meaning the Prime Minister and other Ministers or Members of Parliament - past or present.

Inasmuch as several of the proposed provisions seek to bar the jurisdiction of courts and militate against transparency, freedom of information, freedom of the press, rule of law and equality before law norms, it is extremely doubtful if these will stand judicial scrutiny.

While the 1968 Bill declared that its provisions were to be in addition to the provisions of any other enactment or rule of law under which any remedy was available to the complainant and the Bill did not seek to limit or affect the rights of the complainant to avail of such remedy, the present Bill very specifically bars recourse to all other remedies. Once a complaint is made to the Lokpal, the matter cannot thereafter be referred for inquiry under the Commissions of Inquiry Act 1952 nor can it be taken up in any court of law under public interest litigation or the like as at present.

The most mischievous provision which in combination with the above also gives out perhaps the basic motivation of the proposed Lokpal law and its timing is clause 26 which says that after the Lokpal or the competent authority - Prime Minister or a House of Parliament - to whom Lokpal sends its report holds that allegations of corruption made in a complaint against the Prime Minister, or a Minister or a member of Parliament (present or past) have not been proved, "notwithstanding anything contained in any other law", "no prosecution shall lie on any complaint, report, information or otherwise and no court shall take cognisance of any offence on the basis of the same or substantially the same allegations."

If we would just consider the scenario after this proposed legislation becomes law and comes into force : (1) By the simple device of a complaint being made to the Lokpal, all on-going investigations in cases of corruption against past or present Prime Minister or Ministers or Members of Parliament can be brought to a dead stop; (2) while the Lokpal conducts his *in camera* inquiry, no information about allegations of corruption can be disclosed, printed or published unlike the present position whereunder court proceedings in cases of corruption are being held largely in public and in full glare of publicity with the media freely reporting them; (3) once the Lokpal or the competent authority declares that charges are 'not proved' jurisdiction of all laws and all courts is barred; (4) Unlike the courts that are at present going into cases of corruption, Lokpal would have no powers do itself punish the guilty. Even after the Lokpal reaches the verdict 'guilty' all he can do is to report his findings to the Prime Minister or a House of Parliament, as the case may be. And, who can say that political factors will not influence the final decision at those levels?

Our friends facing corruption charges can hardly ask for anything better than the proposed Lokpal Bill. In the name of fighting corruption at the highest levels, the proposed Bill actually seems to be directed against the present wave of what has come to be called 'judicial activism' and which has made the life of corrupt politicians in all parties miserable. For this reason alone, one would not be surprised if politicians of all hues join together to support this Bill. It may prove to be their ultimate saviour and safeguard against judicial scrutiny of their conduct as public functionaries. Citizens! Beware of the farce and the sinister lullaby of the Lokpal Bill.

ANNEXURE 1

THE LOKPAL BILL, 1996

Bill No.101 of 1996

As Introduced in Lok Sabha on
13th September, 1996

BILL

to provide for the establishment of the institution of Lokpal to inquire into allegations of corruption against public functionaries and for matters connected therewith.

BE it enacted by Parliament in the Forty-Seventh Year of the Republic of India as follows:-

PRELIMINARY

Short title, and commencement.

1. (1) This Act may be called the Lokpal Act, 1996.

(2) It shall come into force on such date as the Central Government may, by notification in the Official Gazette appoint.

Definitions.

2. In this Act, unless the context otherwise requires, —

a) "Chairman" means the Chairman of the Lokpal;

b) "Competent authority", in relation to—

i) the Prime Minister, means the House of the People;

ii) a Member of Council of Ministers other than the Prime Minister, means the Prime Minister;

iii) a Member of Council of Ministers, other than a Minister, means the Council of States in

the case of a Member of that Council and the House of the People in the case of a Member of that House;

c) "Complaint" means a complaint alleging that a public functionary has committed any offence punishable under the Prevention of Corruption Act, 1988; 49 of 1988.

d) "Lokpal" means the institution established under section 3;

e) "Member" means a Member of the Lokpal and includes the Chairman of the Lokpal;

f) "Prescribed" means prescribed by rules made under this Act;

g) "Public functionary" means a person who,-

i) "holds, or has held, the office of the Prime Minister, Minister, Minister of State or Deputy Minister, of the Union;

ii) is, or has been, a Member of either House of Parliament.

MACHINERY FOR INQUIRIES

Establishment of Lokpal

3. (I) As from the commencement of this Act, there shall be established, for the purpose of making inquiries in respect of complaints under this Act, an institution to be called the "Lokpal".

2) the Lokpal shall consist of —

a) a Chairman who is or has been a Chief Justice or Judge of the Supreme Court;

b) two Members who are, or have been, or qualified to be, a judge of the Supreme Court.

3) Every Member shall, before entering upon his office, make and subscribe before the President, or a person appointed in that behalf by the President, an oath or affirmation in the form set out in the Schedule.

Appointment of Chairman and other Members.

4. (1) The Chairman and other Members shall be appointed by the President by warrant under his hand and seal;

Provided that every appointment under this sub-section shall be made after obtaining the recommendations of a Committee consisting of-

a) the Prime Minister - Chairman;

b) Speaker of the House of the People - Member;

c) Minister in-charge of the Ministry of Home Affairs in the Government of India - Member

d) Minister in-charge of the Ministry of Personnel, Public Grievances and Pensions in the Government of India - Member

e) Leader of the Opposition in the House of the people - Member

f) Leader of the Opposition in the Council of States - Member

g) Deputy Chairman of the Council of States - Member

Provided further that no sitting Judge of the Supreme Court or Sitting Justice of a High Court shall be appointed except after consultation with the Chief Justice of India.

2) No appointment of a Chairman or a Member shall be invalid merely by reason of any vacancy in the Committee.

Member to be ineligible to hold other offices.

5. A Member shall not be a Member of Parliament or a Member of the Legislature of any State and shall not hold any office of trust or profit (other than his office as Member), or be connected with any political party, or carry on any business, or practice any profession and accordingly, before he enters upon his office, a person appointed as the Member shall,—

a) if he is a Member of Parliament or of the Legislature of any State, shall resign such membership; or

b) if he holds any office of trust, or profit resign from such office; or

c) if he is connected with any political party, sever his connection with it; or

d) if he is carrying on any business, sever his connection (short of divesting himself of ownership) with the conduct and management of such business; or

e) if he is practicing any profession, cease to practice such profession.

Term of office and other conditions of service of Members.

6. (1) Every Member shall hold office for a term of five years from the date on which he enters

upon his office:

Provided that he may —

a) by writing under his hand addressed to the President, resign his office;

b) be removed from his office in the manner provided in section 7.

(2) On ceasing to hold office, a Member shall be ineligible for further employment to any office of profit under the Government of India or the Government of a State.

3) The salary, allowances and other conditions of service of -

i) the Chairman shall be the same as those of the Chief Justice of India;

ii) other Members shall be the same as those of a Judge of the Supreme Court:

Provided that such salary shall be in addition to any pension to which the Member, may be entitled in respect of any previous service under the Government of India or under the Government of a State and no deduction shall be made from such salary on the ground of his having received any retirement gratuity, or on the ground that he received the commuted value of a portion of the pension, in respect of his previous service:

Provided further that the salary, allowances and pension payable to, and other conditions of service of, a Member shall not be varied to his disadvantage after his appointment.

Removal of a Member

7. A Member shall not be removed from his office except by an order made by the President on the ground of proved misbehaviour or incapacity after an inquiry made by the Chief Justice of India or, as the case may be, by such other Judge of the Supreme Court as the Chief Justice of India may nominate in this behalf, in which the Member had been informed of the charges against him and given a reasonable opportunity of being heard in respect of those charges.

Staff of Lokpal

8. (1) The Lokpal shall, for the purpose of assisting it in the discharge of its functions (including verification and inquiries in respect of

complaints) under this Act, appoint a Secretary and such other officers and employees as the President may determine, from time to time, in consultation with the Lokpal.

(2) Without prejudice to the provisions of sub-section (1), the Lokpal may, for the purpose of dealing with any complaints or any classes of complaints secure—

(i) the services of any officer or employee or investigating agency of the Central Government or a State Government with the concurrence of that Government or

(ii) the services of any other person or agency.

(3) The terms and conditions of service of the officers and employees referred to in sub-section (1) and of the officers, employees, agencies and persons referred to in sub-section (2) (including such special conditions as may be considered necessary for enabling them to act without fear in the discharge of their functions) shall be such as the President may determine, from time to time, in consultation with the Lokpal.

(4) In the discharge of their functions under this Act, the Officers and employees referred to in sub-section (1) and the officers, employees, agencies and persons referred to in sub-section (2) shall be subject to the exclusive administrative control and direction of the Lokpal.

JURISDICTION AND PROCEDURE IN RESPECT OF INQUIRIES

Jurisdiction of Lokpal.

9.(1) Subject to the other provisions of this Act, the Lokpal may inquire into any matter involved in, or arising from, or connected with, any allegation made in a complaint.

(2) The Lokpal may Inquire into any act or conduct of any person other than public functionary in so far as it considers it necessary so to do for the purpose of its inquiry into any such allegation:

Provided that the Lokpal shall give such person a reasonable opportunity of being heard and to produce evidence in his defence.

(3) No matter in respect of which a complaint may be made under this Act shall be referred for inquiry under the Commissions of Inquiry Act, 1952, except on the recommendation, or with the concurrence, of the Lokpal. 60 of 1952

Mattors not subject to jurisdiction of Lokpal

10. (1) The Lokpal shall not inquire into any matter concerning any person if any Member has any bias in respect of such matter or person and if any dispute arises in this behalf, the President shall, on an application made by the party aggrieved, obtain, in such manner as may be prescribed, the opinion of the Chief Justice of India and decide the dispute in conformity with such opinion.

(2) The Lokpal shall not inquire into any matter which has been referred for inquiry under the Commissions of Inquiry Act, 1952, on its recommendation or with its prior concurrence. 60 of 1952

(3) The Lokpal shall not inquire into any complaint if the complaint is made after the expiry of five years from the date on which the offence mentioned in such complaint is alleged to have been committed.

Complaints

11. (1) Any person other than a public servant may make a complaint under this Act to the Lokpal.

Explanation — For the purpose of this sub-section, "public servant" means-

(a) any person who is a member of a Defence service or of a civil service of the Union or a State or of an All India Service or holds any post connected with Defence or any civil post under the Union or a State;

(b) any person in the service or pay of a local authority, a corporation established by or under a Central, Provincial or State Act or a Government company, as defined in section 617 of the Companies Act, 1956. 1 of 1956

(2) The complaint shall be in the prescribed form and shall set forth particulars of the offence alleged and shall be accompanied by fees prescribed, if any, an affidavit in support of such

particulars and a certificate in the prescribed form in respect of the deposit under sub-section (3) or, if the complaint is unable to make the deposit, an application for exemption from the requirement as to such deposit.

(3) The complaint shall deposit in such manner and with such authority or agency as may be prescribed a sum of one thousand rupees to be available for disposal under section 28:

Provided that the Lokpal may, for sufficient cause to be recorded in writing, exempt a complaint from the requirement under this sub-section.

(4) Notwithstanding anything contained in the foregoing sub- sections, any letter written to the Lokpal or, as the case may be, the appropriate authority by a person in any jail or other place of custody or in any asylum or other place for insane persons may, if the Lokpal or, as the case may be, the appropriate authority is satisfied that it is necessary so to do, be treated as a complaint made in accordance with the provisions of this section.

(5) Notwithstanding anything contained in any other enactment, it shall be the duty of a police officer or other person in charge of any jail or other place of custody or of any asylum or other place for insane persons to forward, without opening, any letter addressed to the Lokpal or the appropriate authority by a person imprisoned or detained in such jail, place of custody, asylum or other place, to the Lokpal or the appropriate authority without delay.

Explanation - "appropriate authority" means any of the authorities which the Lokpal may, by general or special order, in writing, determine to be appropriate authorities for the purposes of this section.

Preliminary scrutiny of complaints by Lokpal.

12. (1) If the Lokpal is satisfied after considering a complaint and after making such verification as it deems appropriate, -

(a) that the complaint is not made within the period of five years' specified in sub-section (3) of section 10; or

(b) that it cannot make an inquiry in respect of the complaint by reason of the provisions of sub-section (1) or sub-section (2) of section 10 or any other provision of this Act, or

c) that the complaint is frivolous or vexatious or is not made in good faith; or

(d) that there are no sufficient grounds for inquiring into the complaint,

the Lokpal shall dismiss the complaint after recording its reasons therefor and communicate the same to the complaints and to the competent authority.

(2) The procedure for verification in respect of a complaint under sub-section (1) shall be such as the Lokpal deems appropriate in the circumstances of the case and in particular the Lok Pal may, if it deems it necessary so to do, call for the comments of the public functionary concerned.

Procedure in respect of inquiries.

13. (1) If, after the consideration and verification under section 12 in respect of a complaint, the Lokpal proposes to conduct any inquiry, it—

a) shall forthwith forward a copy of the complaint to the competent authority;

b) may make such orders as to the safe custody of documents relevant to the inquiry as it deems fit;

c) shall, at such time as it considers appropriate, forward a copy of the complaint to the public, functionary concerned and afford him an opportunity to present his case.

(2) Every such inquiry shall be conducted in camera by the Chairman and the Members sitting jointly.

(3) The Lokpal shall hold every such inquiry as expeditiously as possible and in any case complete the inquiry within a period of six months from the date of receipt of the complaint :

Provided that the Lokpal may for reasons to be recorded in writing may complete the inquiry within a further period of six months.

(4) Save as aforesaid, the procedure for conducting any such inquiry shall be such as the Lokpal considers appropriate in the circumstances of the case.

Power of Lokpal to issue, in certain circumstances, directions for deferring or suspending investigation into an offence.

14. (1) Where the Lokpal is satisfied —

(a) that investigation by any police officer
2 of 1974 under the Code of Criminal Procedure 1973, into any offence in respect of which a complaint is made or into any matters connected therewith may prejudicial affect the conduct of inquiry under this Act with respect to such complaint, and

(b) that having regard to all the circumstances of the case it would be proper to defer such investigation pending the completion of such inquiry.

it may, by order in writing and for reasons to be recorded therein, direct that till the completion of such inquiry or for such shorter period as may be specified in the order any such investigation shall be deferred or, as the case may be shall be suspended.

Provided that no such direction shall apply with respect to any investigation required to be made in pursuance of an order of any court.

(2) Notwithstanding anything contained in the
2 of 1974 Code of Criminal Procedure, 1973, in computing, for the purposes of Chapter XXXVI of that Code, the period of limitation for taking cognizance of any offence, being an offence the investigation in respect of which has been deferred or suspended by reason of an order under sub-section (1), the date on which such order was made, the period during which the investigation remained deferred, or as the case may be suspended by reason of the order and the date on which the order ceased to have effect, shall be excluded.

Evidence

15. (1) Subject to the provisions of this section, for the purpose of any inquiry (including the verification under section (12), the Lokpal—

(a) may require any public servant or any other person, who, in its opinion is able to furnish information or produce documents relevant to such inquiry, to furnish any such information or produce any such document;

(b) shall have all the powers of a civil court while trying a suit under the Code of Civil Procedure, 1908, in respect of the following 5 of 1908 matters, namely :-

(i) Summoning and enforcing the attendance of any person an examining him on oath;

(ii) requiring the discovery and production of any document;

(iii) receiving evidence on affidavits;

(iv) requisitioning any public record or copy thereof from any court or office;

(v) issuing commissions for the examination of witnesses or documents, and

(vi) such other matters as may be prescribed.

(2) A proceeding before the Lokpal shall be 45 of 1860 deemed to be a judicial proceeding within the meaning of section 193 of the Indian Penal Code.

(3) Subject to the provisions of sub-section (4), —

(a) no obligation to maintain secrecy or other restriction upon the disclosure of information obtained or furnished to Government or any public servant, whether imposed by any enactment or by any provisions of law whatever shall apply to the disclosure of information for the purpose of any inquiry (including the verification, under section (12) under this Act, and

(b) the Government or any public servant shall not be entitled, in relation to any such verification or inquiry, to any such privilege in respect of the production of documents or the giving of evidence as is allowed by any enactment or by any provisions of law whatever in legal proceedings.

(4) No person shall be required or authorised by virtue of this Act to furnish any such information or answer any such question or produce so much of any document-

(a) as might prejudice the security, or defence, or international relations of India (including India's relations, with the Government of any other country or with any international organisation), or the investigation or detection of crime; or

(b) as might involve the disclosure of proceedings of the Cabinet of the union Government or of any Committee of such Cabinet; Cabinet of the State Government or of any Committee of such Cabinet, and for the purpose of this sub-section, a certificate issued by a Secretary to the Government of India or Chief Secretary of the State Government, as the case may be, certifying that any information, answer, or portion of a document, is of the nature specified in clause (a) or clause (b) shall be binding and conclusive:

Provided that the Lokpal may require any information or answer or portion of a document in respect of which a certificate is issued under this sub-section to the effect that it is of the nature specified in clause (a) to be disclosed to it

Explanation- For the purpose of this section, "public servant' shall have the same meaning as in section 21 of the Indian Penal Code. 45 of 1860

Search and seizure

16. (1) If the Lokpal has reason to believe that any documents which, in its opinion, will be useful for, or relevant to, any inquiry under this Act, are secreted in any place, it may authorise any officer subordinate to it, or any officer of an investigating agency referred to in sub-section (2) of section 8, to search for and to seize such documents.

(2) If the Lokpal is satisfied that any documents seized under sub-section (1) would be evidence for the purpose of any inquiry under this Act and that it would be necessary to retain the document in its custody, it may so retain the said document till the completion of such inquiry:

Provided that where such documents is seized before the commencement of such inquiry, the Lokpal shall return the document before the expiration of a period of one year from the date on which it is seized unless such inquiry has been commenced before such expiration.

Explanation.—For the purposes of this sub-section, an inquiry in respect of a complaint—

(a) shall be deemed to have commenced on the date on which the Lokpal forwards a copy of the competent authority under clause (a) of sub-section (1) of section 13;

(b) shall be deemed to have been completeu on the date on which the Lokpal closes the case uder clause (a) of sub-section (1) of section 17 or where the Lokpal makes a report to the competent authority under clause (b) of that sub-section, on the expiry of the period mentioned in sub-section (3) of that section.

(3) The provisions of the Code of Criminal Procedure, 1973, relating to searches shall, so far as may be, apply to searches under this section subject to te modification that sub-section (5) of section 165 of the said Code shall have effect as if, for the word "Magistrate", wherever it occurs, the words "Lokpal or any officer authorised by it" were substituted. 2 of 1974

Reports

17. (1) If, after inquiry in respect of a complaint, the Lokpal is satisfied that—

(a) no allegation made in the complaint has been substantiated either wholly or party, it shall close the case ad intimate the complainant authority accordingly;

(b) all or any of the allegations made in the complaint have or has been substantiated either wholly or partly, it shall by report in writing, communicate its findings and recommendations to the competent authority and intimate te complaintant and the public functionary about its having made the report.

(2) The competent authority in the case of a public functionary, other than the Prime Minister, shall examine the report forwarded to it under clause (b) of sub-seection (1) and communicate to the Lokpal, within three months of the date of receipt of report, the action taken or proposed to be taken on the basis of the report.

(3) The Speaker, in the case of the Prime Minister or a Member of the House of the People and the Chairman of the Council of States in the case of a Member of that Council shall, as soon as may be after and in anycase not later than ninety days from the receipt of report under clause

(b) of sub-section (1), cause the same to be laid before the House of the People or the Council of States, as the case may be.

Explanation.—In computing the period of ninety days referred to in this sub-section, any period during which the House of the People or the Council of States, as the case may be is not in session shall be excluded.

(4) The Lokpal shall present annually to the President a consolidated report on the administration of this Act and the President shall, as soon as may be after, and in any case not later than ninety days from the receipt of such report, cause the same, together with an explanatory memorandum, to be laid before each House of Parliament.

Explanation.—In computing the period of ninety days referred to in this sub-section, any period during which Parliament or, as the casemay be, either House of Parliament, is not in session, shall be exluded.

DECLARATION OF ASSETS AND LIABILITIES

Declaration of assets by Members of Parliament.

18. Every Member of Parliament shall furnish a return of all assets owned by him and members of his family and all liabilities incurred by him and the members of his family before Lokpal every year in such form as may be prescribed.

MISCELLANEOUS

Expenditure on Members to be charnged on the Consolidated Fund of India.

19. The salaries, allowance and pensions payable to, or in respect of, the Members, shall be expenditure charged on the Consolidated Fund of India.

Secrecy of information.

1 of 1872

20 (1) Any information obtained by the Lokpal, or by any officer, employee, agency or person referred to in section 8, in the course of, or for the purposes of, any verification or inquiry under this Act, and any evidence recorded or collected in connection therewith shall be treated as confidential and, nothwithstanding anything contained in the Indian Evidence Act, 1872, no court shall be entitled to compel the Lokpal, or any such officer, employee, agency or person, to give evidence relating to such information or to produce the evidence so recorded or collected.

(2) Nothing in sub-section (1) shall apply to the disclosure of the information or evidence referred to therein—

(a) for the purposes of this Act or for the purposes of any action or proceedings to be taken on any report under section 17; or

(b) for the purposes of any proceeedings, for an offence of giving or fabricating false evidence, 45 of 1860
under the Indian Penal Code; or

(c) for such other purposes as may be prescribed.

International insult, or interruption to, or bringing into disrepute, Lokpal.

International insult, or interruption to, or bringing into disrepute, Lokpal.

21. (1) Whoever intentionally offers any insult, or causes any interruption, to the Lokpal while the Lokpal or any of its Members is making any verification or conducting any inquiry under this Act, shall be punished with simple imprisonment for a term which may extend to six months, or with fine, or with both.

(2) Whoever, by words spoken or intended or intended to be read, makes or pulishes any statement, or does any other act, which is calculated to bring the Lokpal into disrepute, shall be punished with simple imprisonment for a term which may extend to six months, or with fine, or with both.

(3) The provisions of sub-section (2) of section 199 of the Code of Criminal Procedure, 1973, shall apply in relation to an offence under 2 of 1974
sub-section (1) or sub-section (2) as they apply in relation to an offence referred to in sub-section (2) of the said section 199, subject to the modification that no complaint in respect of such offence shall be made by the Public Prosecutor except with the previous sanction of the Lokpal.

Power of Lokpal to try certain offences summarily.

22. (1) If, at any stage of a proceeding before the Lokpal, it appears to the Lokpal that any person appearing in such proceedings had knowingly or wilfully given false evidence or had fabricated false evidence with the intention that
2 of 1974 such evidence should be used in such proceedings,
the Lokpal may, if satisfied that it is necessary and expedient in the interests of justice that the person should be tried summarily for giving or fabricating, as the case may be, false evidence, take cognizance of the offence and may, after giving the offender a reasonable opportunity of showing cause why he should not be punished for such offence, try such offender summarily, so far as may be, in accordance with the procedure prescribed for summary trials under the Code of Criminal Procedure, 1973, and sentence him to simple imprisonment for a term which may extend to one month, or to fine which may extend to five hundred rupees, or to both.

(2) When any such offence as is described in section 175, section 178, section 179 or section
45 of 1860 180 of the Indian Penal Code is committed in the
view or presence of the Lokpal, the Lokpal may cause the offender to be detailed in custody and
2 of 1974 may, at any time on the same day, take cognizance
of the offence and, after giving the offender a reasonable opportunity of showing cause why he should not be punished under this section, try such offender summarily so far as may be in accordance with the procedure prescribed for summary trails the Code of Criminal Procedure, 1973 and sentence him to simple imprisonment for a term which may extend to one month, or to fine which may extend to five hundred rupees, or to both.

(3) In every case tried under this section, the Lokpal shall record the facts constituting the offence with the statement (if any) made by the offender as well as the finding and the sentence.

(4) Any person convicted on a trial held under this section may appeal to the High Court and the
2 of 1974 provisions of Chapter XXIX of the Code of
Criminal Procedure, 1973, shall so far as may be,

apply to appeals under this section and the High Court may alter or reverse the finding, or reduce or reverse the sentence appealed against.

Explanation.—For the purposes of this sub-section, "High Court" means the High Court within the jurisdiction of which the person convicted ordinarily resides or carries on business or personally works for gains or the High Court within whose jurisdiction the order of conviction has been passed.

(5) The provisions of this section shall have effect notwithstanding anything contained in the Code of Criminal Procedure, 1973. 2 of 1974

Disclosure of information and publiction of false information in respect of complaints and proceedings under this Act.

23.(1) If any person prints or publishes any information with respect to any complaint under this Act (including the identity of the person making the complaint, the public functionary against whom the complaint has been made and the particulars contained in the complaint) or with respect to any proceeding, act or thing taken or done or purported to have been taken or done under this Act in relation to such complaint,—

(a) where the Lokpal dismisses such complaint under section 12, at any time before such dismissal; or

(b) where the Lokpal closes the case with respect to such complaint under clause (a) of sub-section (1) of section 17, at any time before such closure; or

(c) where the Lokpal forwards to the competent authority a report of its findings and recommendations with respect to such complaint under clause (b) of sub-section (1) of section 17, at any time before the expiry of three months from the date of receipt of the report by the competent authority, or as the case may be, at any time before the report is laid before the House of the People or the Council of States under sub-section (3) of section 17, such person shall be guilty of an offence under this sub section.

(2) If any person prints or publishes any information alleging or suggesting that a complaint has been made under this Act against

any public functionary and such information is false, such person shall be guilty of an offence under this sub-section.

(3) When any offence under sub-section (1) or sub-section (2) is committed, the Lokpal may take cognizance of the offence and, after giving the offender reasonable opportunity of showing cause why he should not be punished for such offence, try such offender summarily so far as may be in accordance with the procedure prescribed for summary trials under the Code of Criminal
2 of 1974 Procedure, 1973 and sentence him to imprisonment for a term which may extend to six months, or to fine which may extend to ten thousand rupees, or to both.

(4) In every case tried under this section, the Lokpal shall record the facts constituting the offence with the statement (if any) made by the offender as well as the findings and the sentence.

(5) Any person convicted in a trial under this section may with the leave of the Supreme Court, prefer an appeal to the Supreme Court within thirty days of such conviction or within such further period as the Supreme Court may for sufficient cause allow and, save as aforesaid, no appeal or revision shall lie in any court against such conviction.

(6) the provisions of this section shall have
2 of 1974 effect notwithstanding anything contained in the Code of Criminal procedure, 1973.

Action in case of false complaints.

24. (1) Every person who makes any complaint which is held by the Lokpal to be false shall be punishable as provided in sub-section (2).

(2) When any offence under sub-section (1) is committed, the Lokpal may take cognizance of the offence and after giving the offender a reasonable opportunity of showing cause why he should not be punished for such offence, try such
2 of 1974 offender summarily, so far as may be, in accordance with the procedure prescribed for summary trials under the Code of Criminal Procedure, 1973 and sentence him to imprisonment for a term which shall be not be less than one

year but which may extend to three years and also to fine which may be extend to fifth thousand rupees and may also award, out of the amount of fine, to the public functionary against whom such false complaint has been made, such amount of compensation as the Lokpal thinks fit.

(3) In every case tried under this section, the Lokpal shall record the facts constituting the offence with the statement (if any) made by the offender as well as the findings and the sentence.

(4) Any person convicted on a trial under this section may, with the leave of the Supreme Court, prefer an appeal to the Supreme Court within thirty days of such conviction or within such further period as the Supreme Court may for sufficient cause allow and, save as aforesaid, no appeal or revision shall lie in court against such conviction.

(5) The provisions of this section shall have effect notwithstanding anything contained in the Code of Criminal Procedure, 1973. 2 of 1974

Application of Act 2 of 1974.

25. Subject to the other provisions of this Act and subject to the modification that for purpose of transfer of any case under section 23 or section 24, the provisions of section 406 of the Code of Criminal Procedure, 1973, shall alone apply, the provisions of the said Code shall apply to proceedings before a Lokpal under section 22, 23 and 24 and for the purposes of the said provisions of that Code and the said proceedings the Lokpal shall be deemed to be a Court of Session and shall have all the powers of a Court of Session.

Bar of prosecution on allegations not proved or not substantiated.

26. Notwithstanding anything contained in any other law for the time being in force, where on an inquiry in respect of a complaint against a public functionary the Lokpal or the competent authority has held that any allegations made in the complaint have not been proved or substantiated, no prosecution shall lie on any complaint, report, information or otherwise and no court shall take cognizance of any offence on the basis of the same or substantially the same allegations as in the complaint.

Conferment of additional functions of Lokpal.

27. (1) The President may, by order in writing and subject to such conditions or limitations as

may be specified in the order, require the Lokpal to inquire into any allegation (being an allegation in respect of which a complaint may be made) specified in the order in respect of a public functionary and, notwithstanding anything contained in this Act, the Lokpal shall comply with such order.

(2) When the Lokpal is to make any inquiry under sub-section (1), the Lokpal shall exercise the same powers and discharge the same functions as it would in the case of any inquiry made on a complaint under this Act and the provisions of this Act (except section 24) shall apply accordingly.

Disposal of deposit.

28. The sum deposited by a complainant under section 11 shall —

(a) in a case where the complaint is dismissed under clause (c) of sub-section (1) of section 12, stand forfeited to the Central Government;

(b) if the Lokpal, for reasons to be recorded in writing so directs, be utilised for compensating the public functinary complained against; and

(c) in any other case, be refunded to the complainant.

Compensation or reward, for both, payable in certain cases to complainant

Compensation or reward, for both, payable in certain cases to complainant.

29. If the Lokpal is satisfied—

(a) that all or any of the allegations made in a complaint have or has been substantiated either wholly or partly; and

(b) that having regard to the expenses incurred by the complaint in relation to the proceedings in respect of such complaint and all other relevant circumstances of the case the complainant deserves to be compensated or rewarded, the Lokpal shall determine the amount which shall be paid to the complainant by way of such compensation or reward and the Central Government shall pay, the amount or amounts so determined, to the complainant.

Protection of action taken in good faith.

30.(1) No suit, prosecution or other legal proceedings shall lie against the Lokpal or against any officer, employee, agency or person referred to in section 8, in respect of anything which is in good faith done, or intended to be done, under this Act.

(2) Save as otherwise provided in this Act, no proceedings or decisions of the Lokpal shall be liable to be challenged, reviewed, quashed or called in question in any Court.

Power to delegate.

31. The Lokpal may, by general or special order in writing, and subject to such conditions and limitations as may be specified therein, direct that any powers conferred or duties imposed on it by or under this Act [except the powers under the proviso to sub-section (3) of section 11, the power to dismiss a complaint under sub-section (1) of section 12, the powers to close cases and make reports under section 17 and the powers under sections 22, 23 and 24] may also be exercised or discharged by such of the officers, employees or agencies referred to in sub-section (1) of sub-section (2) of section 8, as may be specified in the order.

Power to make rules.

32(1) The President may, by notification in the Official Gazette, make rules for the purpose of carrying into effect the provisions of this Act.

(2) In particular, and without prejudice to the generality of the foregoing provisions, such rules may provide for—

(a) the manner in which the President shall obtain the opinion of the Chief Justice of India under sub-section (1) of section 10;

(b) the form in which complaints may be made under sub-section (1) of section 11 and the fees, if any, which may be charged in respect thereof;

(c) the manner in which and the authorities or agencies with whom deposits shall be made under sub-section (3) of section 11 and the form in which certificates shall be furnished in respect of such deposits;

(d) the matters referred to in sub-clause (vi) of clause (b) of sub-section (1) of section 15;

(e) the form in which return has to be furnished under section 18;

(f) the purposes referred to in clause (c) of sub-section (2) of section 20;

(g) any other matter which is to be or may be prescribed.

(3) Every rule made under this Act shall be laid, as soon as may be after it is made, before each House of Parliament; while it is in session, for a total period of thirty days which may be comprised in one session or in two or more successive sessions, and if, before the expiry of the session immediately following the session or the successive sessions aforesaid, both Houses agree in making any modification in the rule, or both Houses agree that the rule should not be made, the rule shall thereafter have effect only in such modified form or be of no effect, as the case may be; so, however, that any such modification or annulment shall be without prejudice to the validity of anything previously done under that rule.

33. For the removal of doubts, it is hereby declared that nothing in this Act shall operate to confer ro enable the conferring of any jurisdiction on the Lokpal to make any inquiry- Removal of doubts.

(a) into any allegation against or any act or conduct of—

(i) the President, the Vice-President or the Speaker of the House of the People;

(ii) the Chief Justice or any other Judge of the Supreme Court of India;

(iii) the Comptroller and Auditor-General of India, the Chief Election Commissioner or other Election Commissioner or the Chairman or any other Member of the Union Public Service Commission;

(b) upon its own knowledge or information.

34. Nothing contained in this Act shall be construed as affecting the constitution of, or the Saving.
60 of 1952. continuance of functioning or exercise of powers by, any Commission of Inquiry appointed under the Commissions of Inquiry Act, 1952 before the commencement of this Act and no complaint shall be made under this Act in respect of any matter referred for inquiry to such Commission before such commencement.

Consequential amendment of Act 60 of 1952.

35. In section 3 of the Commissions of Inquiry Act, 1952, in sub-section (1), for the words "The appropriate Government may", the words, brackets and figures "subject to the provisions of sub-section (3) of section 9 of the Lokpal Act, 1966, the appropriate Government" shall be substituted.

THE SCHEDULE

[See Section 3(3)]

1,____________________ having been appointed Chairman/Member of the Lokpal do swear in the name of God'solemnly affirm that I will bear true faith and allegiance to the constitution of India as by law established, that I will duly and faithfully and to the best of my ability, knowledge and judgment perform the duties of my office without fear or favour, affection or ill-will.

STATEMENT OF OBJECTS AND REASONS

In its iterim report on the "Problem of Redress of Citizens' Grievances" submitted in 1966, the Administrative Reforms Commission recommended, inter alia, the setting up of an institution of Lokpal.

2. To give efforts to this recommendation of the Administration Reforms Commission, a Bill called the "Lokpal and the Lokayuktas Bill, 1968" was introduced in the Fourth Lok Sabha in 1968. The Bill was considerably by a Joint Committee of the two Houses of Parliament and the Bill, as reported by the Joint Committee, was passed by the Lok Sabha in 1969. While this Bill was pending in Rajya Sabha, the Fourth Lok Sabha was dissolved and consequently, the Bill lapsed. In 1971, the Bill passed by the previous Lok Sabha was reintroduced in the Lok Sabha as the "Lokpal and Lokayuktas Bill, 1971". This Bill also lapsed on the dissolution of the Fifth Lok Sabha.

3. A fresh Bill called the "Lokpal Bill, 1977" was introduced in the Lok Sabha in 1977. This Bill was referred to a Joint Committee of both the Houses of Parliament which submitted its report in July, 1978. When the Bill, as reported by the Joint Committee, was under consideration of the Lok Sabha, the Lok Sabha was prorogued and was subsequently dissolved. Consequently that Bill also lapsed.

4. The Lokpal Bill, 1985 was introduced in the Lok Sabha and subsequently withdrawn. The Lokpal Bill, 1989 which sought to include the office of Prime Minister also within the jurisdiction of the Lokpal which was to be a three Member body lapsed with the dissolution of the Lok Sabha.

5. The Lokpal Bill, 1966 provides for setting up the office of Lokpal with a Chairman and two Members for a fixed tenure. With a view to ensuring that the Lokpal is able to act independently and discharge its functions without fear or favour, the Bill provides that the Chairman/ Member of Lokpal shall not be removed from his office except by an order made by the President on the ground of proved misbehaviour or incapacity after an inquiry made by the Chief Justice of India or by any other Judge of the Supreme Court nominated by the Chief Justice of India for this purpose. It is also provided that the Chairman and other Members of a Committee consisting of Prime Minister as Chairman, Speaker Lok Sabha, Deputy Chairman Rajya Sabha, Leaders of the Opposition in the Lok Sabha/ Rajya Sabha, Minister-in-charge of the Ministry of Home Affairs and Minister of State, Ministry of Personnel and Public Grievances and Pensions as Members. Under the scheme of the Bill, the Lokpal will inquire into complaints alleging that a public functionary as defined in the Bill has committed an offence punishable under the Prevention of Corruption Act, 1988 and the expression "public functionary" covers, Prime Minister, Minister, Ministers of State, Deputy Ministers and Members' of Parliament. It seeks to carry out in this respect the object and purpose of the recommendations of the Administrative Reforms Commission for enabling the citizen to have recourse to a convenient and effective forum for determination of complaints and thereby save him from pursuing his remedy through the process of Courts, which may prove expensive or dilatory and may not facilitate in speedy determination. The Bill also seeks to make special provisions for discouraging frivolous, vexatious and false complaints. The bill also provides for declaration of assets and liabilities by Members of Parliament and their family members, annually. The Notes on clauses explain the provisions contained in the Bill.

6. The Bill seeks to achieve the above objects.

NEW DELHI: S.R-BALASUBRAMONIYAN
The 10th September, 1996

Notes on clauses

Clause 2 defines the various expressions used in the Bill.

Clause 3 provides for the establishment of Lokpal consisting of a Chairman and two Members. The person to be appointed as Chairman will be a person who is or has been the Chief Justice of India or a Judge of the Supreme Court. Member shall be a person who is, or has been or is qualified to be a Judge of that Court.

Clause 4 provides that the Chairman and other Members shall be appointed after obtaining the recommendations of a Committee consisting of the Prime Minister. Speaker of the House of the People, Home Minister, Leaders of the Opposition in the House of the People and the Council of States, the Deputy Chairman of the Council of States and the Minister in-charge of Ministry of Personnel.

Clause 5 is self-explanatory.

Clause 6 provides for the term of office conditions of service of the Chairman or Members of Lokpal. His conditions of service, salary, allowances and pension of the Chairman will be the same as those of Chief Justice of India. The salary of the member will be in addition to any pension which he might be entitled to in respect of any previous service under the Government of India or under the Government of a State, and no deduction will also be made in regard to any retirement gratuity or commuted value of pension in respect of his previous service. After a person is appointed as Member, his conditions of service, allowances and pension payable to him shall not be varied to his disadvantages.

Clause 7 deals with the removal of a Member.

Clause 8 deals with the staff of the Lokpal and the powers of the Lokpal to utilise the services, inter alia, of any investigating agencies of Government and of any other agencies.

Clause 9 deals with the jurisdiction of the lokpal. Sub-clause (1) provides that the Lokpal may inquire into any matter involved in, or arising from, or connected with any allegation made in a complaint. Sub-clause (2) provides that the Lokpal may conduct an inquiry into any act or conduct of any person other than the public functionary concerned if it considers necessary to do so far the purposes of his inquiry into any allegation. Sub-clause (3) provides that an inquiry under the Commissions of Inquiry Act, 1952 cannot be made in respect of a matter in respect of which a complaint has been made to the Lokpal except on the recommendation or with the concurrence of the Lokpal.

Clause 10 provides that Lokpal shall not inquire into any matter in respect of any person if he has any bias in respect of such person or matter, or into any matter which has been referred for inquiry under the Commissions of Inquiry Act, 1952, on its recommendation or with its prior concurrence. It also provides that Lokpal shall not inquire into any complaint made after a period of five years from the date of the Commission of the offence mentioned in the complaint.

Clause 11 provides that any person that than a public servant as defined therein can file a complaint which shall be in prescribed form and shall be accompanied by an affidavit. This clause also provides for a deposit of Rs.1,000 by the complainant.

Clause 12 provides for preliminary scrutiny of complaints by the Lokpal.

Clause 13 provides for the procedure for making inquiries into the complaints by the Lokpal. It also provides that the Lokpal shall complete the inquiry within six months from the date of the receipt of the complaint.

Clause 14 provides for deferment or for suspension for a specified period or till the completion of inquiry by the Lokpal of any investigation or inquiry by any police officer under the Code of Criminal Procedure, 1973, in respect of matters connected with a complaint being inquired into by the Lokpal by an order and for the reasons to be recorded. However, the Lokpal cannot give such a direction in respect of any investigation to be made in pursuance of an order of any Court. Sub-clause (2) of this clause also provides that for the purposes of Chapter XXXVI of the Code of Criminal procedure, 1973, the period of deferment or suspension of any investigation into an offence will be excluded from the period of limitation for taking cognizance of the offence.

Sub-clause (1) of Clause 15 deals with the powers of the Lokpal to require any public servant to furnish any information or produce any document. Sub-clause (2) provides that the proceedings before the Lokpal shall be deemed to be judicial proceedings within the meaning of section 193 of the Code of Criminal Procedure, 1973.

Clause 16 seeks to confer powers of search and seizure on the Lokpal.

Clause 17 relates to reports of the Lokpal and action thereon. Sub-clause(1) provides that when after inquiry no allegation made in the complaint in substantiated, the Lokpal shall close the case and intimate the complainant, the public functionary and the competent authority accordingly. When all or any of the allegations made in the complaint are substantiated, the Lokpal will made a report communicating its findings and recommendations to the competent authority and will also intimate the complainant as well as public functionary about his having made the report. Sub-clause (2) provides that the competent authority will inform the Lokpal of the action taken or proposed to be taken on the report within a period of three months. Sub-clause(3) provides for the presentation by the Lokpal of annual reports on the administration of the Act to the President and for the laying of such reports before the Houses of Parliament.

Clause 18 provides for declaration of assets by Members of Parliament.

Clause 19 provides that the salaries, allowances and pension payable to the Members of Lokpal shall be charged on the Consolidated Fund of India.

Clause 20 provides for secrecy of information and evidence collected during any inquiry by Lokpal.

Clause 21 provides for punishment for intentional insult or interruption to, or bringing into disrepute the Lokpal.

Clause 22 seeks to confer powers on the Lokpal to try summarily and punish persons giving false evidence, etc., in any proceedings before the Lokpal or committing offences under section 175, 178, 179 or 180 of the

Indian Penal Code in view or the presence of the member. The clause provides that a person convicted thereunder may prefer an appeal to the High Court within the jurisdiction of which the person convicted ordinarily resides or carries on business or personally works for gain or the High Court within whose jurisdiction the order of conviction has been passed.

Clause 23 provides for the disclosure of information in respect of complaints against public functionary or proceedings relating thereto causes irreparable damage to the public functionary in those cases where the public functionary has been absolved of the charges against him. This clause accordingly makes printing or publication of any such information in relation to any complaint before the inquiry under the Act has reached a definitive stage on offence triable summarily by the Lokpal. The clause also seeks to make the printing or publishing of any false information alleging or suggesting that a complaint has been made against a public functionary or offence triable summarily by the Lokpal. The clause also provides that an appeal against any conviction for any offence thereunder may be made to the Supreme Court of India with the leave of that Court.

Clause 24 provides for the punishment which may be awarded by the Lokpal to a person making a complaint which is found by the Lokpal to be false. The clause also provides that any person convicted thereunder may, with the leave of the Supreme Court, prefer an appeal to that Court.

Clause 25 provides for the modified application of the provisions of the code of Criminal Procedure for the trial of offences under sections 22, 23 and 24.

Clause 26 provides for bar of prosecution on allegations not proved or not substantiated before the Lokpal.

Clause 27 relates to conferment of certain additional functions on the Lokpal.

Clause 28 provides for the disposal of deposits made by the complainants.

Clause 29 provides for compensation or reward or both payable to complainant in the event of all or any of the allegations made in a complaint being substantiated.

Clause 30 provides for protection from legal proceedings, etc.

Clause 31 provides for delegation of powers by the Lokpal to its staff, etc.

Clause 32 provides for the power of the President to make rules.

Clause 33 seeks to make it clear that the Lokpal shall not have any jurisdiction to conduct any inquiry into any allegation against or any act or conduct of the President, the vice-President or the Speaker of the House of the People, the Chief Justice or any other judge of the Supreme Court of India, the Comptroller and Auditor-General of India, the Chief Election Commissioner or other Election Commissioners or the Chairman or any other Member of the Union Public Service Commission or to make any inquiry suo-moto.

Clause 34 provides that the provisions of this Bill shall not affect the constitution or the continuance of any Commission of Inquiry appointed under the Commissions of Inquiry Act, 1952 before the coming into force of the provisions of this Bill.

Clause 35 seeks to make a consequential amendment in the Commissions of Inquiry Act, 1952.

FINANCIAL MEMORANDUM

Clause 3(1) of the Bill provides for the appointment of the Lokpal consisting of a Chairman and two other Members. Clause 6(3) of the Bill envisages that the salary, allowances and all other conditions of service of, the Chairman shall be the same as those of the Chief Justice of India and the Members as those of the judge of the Supreme Court. It also provides that the salary payable to the Members shall be in addition to any pension and pension equivalent of other pensionary benefits to which the Member may be be entitled to in respect of any previous service under the Government of India or under the Government of a State.

2. Sub-clause (1) of clause 8 provides that the Lokpal shall appoint a Secretary and such other officers and employees as the President may determine, from time to time, in consultation with Lokpal to assist him in the discharge of his functions. Sub-clause (2) of clause 8 empowers the Lokpal to secure for the purpose of dealing with any complaints or any classes of complaints, the services of any officer or employee or investigating agency of the Central Government or a State Government or the service of any other person or agency. Sub-clause (3) of clause 8 provides that the terms and conditions of service of the officers and employees of the Lokpal and of the officers, employees, agencies and persons referred to in-sub-clause (2) of that clause shall be such as the President may determine in consultation with the Lokpal.

3. Clause 19 of the Bill provides that the expenditure on the salaries, allowances and pensions payable to Members shall be charged on or in respect of the Consolidated Fund of India.

4. Clause 29 of the Bill provides for payment of compensation or reward to a complainant as determined by the Lokpal, by the Central Government.

5. At this stage, it is not possible to give precise details of the expenditure to be incurred on the Lokpal. It is however, expected that the Bill, when enacted, will involve a non-recurring expenditure of Rs.25 lakhs and a recurring expenditure of Rs.1 crore a year. In case it becomes necessary construct a building to house the establishment of the Lokpal,

additional expenditure of a non-recurring nature of the order of Rs. 1crore may also be involved.

The Bill if enacted will not incur any other recurring or non-recurring expenditure.

MEMORANDUM REGARDING DELEGATED LEGISLATION

Clause 32 of the Bill empowers the President to make rules for the purpose of carrying into effect the provisions of proposed enactment. The various matters in relation to which such rules may be made have been enumerated in detail under various items of sub-clause (2) of that clause and relate mainly to the form in which complaints may be made and the fees, if any which may be charged in respect thereof; the manner in which and the authorities or agencies with whom deposits shall be made under sub-clause (3) of clause 11 and the form in which certificate shall be furnished in respect of such deposits under sub-clause (2) of clause 11; and the additional matters in respect of which powers of a civil court may be exercised by the Lokpal. These are matters of detail necessary for effective administration of the provisions of the Bill and it is difficult to provide for all the situations in the Bill itself. The delegation of legislative power is, therefore, of a normal character.

ANNEXURE

EXTRACT FROM THE COMMISSION OF INQUIRY ACT, 1952 (60 OF 1952)

3. (1) The appropriate Government may, if it is of opinion that it is necessary so to do, and shall, if a resolution in this behalf is passed by the House of the People or, as the case may be, the Legislative Assembly of the State, by notification in the Official Gazette, appoint a Commission of Inquiry for the purpose of making an inquiry into any definite matter of public importance and performing such functions and within such time as may be specified in the notification, and the Commission so appointed shall make the inquiry and perform the functions accordingly:

Provided that where any such Commission has been appointed to inquire into any matter —

(a) by the Central Government, no State Government shall, except with the approval of the Central Government, appoint another Commission to inquire into the same matter for long as the Commission appointed by the Central Government is functioning;

(b) by a State Government, the Central Government shall not appoint another Commission to inquire into the same matter for so long as the Commission appointed by the State Government is functioning, unless the Central Government is of opinion that the scope of the inquiry should be extended to two or more States.

ANNEXURE 2

REPORT OF THE PARLIAMENTARY STANDING COMMITTEE ON HOME AFFAIRS ON THE LOKPAL BILL, 1996

1. the Chairman of the Committee on Home Affairs, having been authorised by the Committee to present the Report on its behalf, present this Fortieth Report of the Committee, relating to the Lokpal Bill, 1996.

2. In pursuance of the Rules relating to the Department-related Parliamentary Standing Committees, the Chairman, Rajya Sabha, in consultation with the Speaker, Lok Sabha referred the Lokpal Bill, 1996, as introduced in the Lok Sabha on the 13th September, 1996 and pending therein, to the Committee for examination and Report.

3. The institution of Lokpal, as the Statement of Objects and Reasons appended to the Bill says, has been sought to be established on the basis of the recommendations of the Administrative Reforms Commission (ARC) contained in its interim Report on the "Problem of Redress of Citizens' Grievances". This Report of the ARC was submitted in 1966 and the earlier attempts at legislation for setting up such an institution could not fructify in 1968, 1971, 1977, 1985 and 1989 for various reasons. The current Bill, as the Statement of Objects and Reasons goes on to say, seeks to carry out the object and purpose of the recommendations of ARC for enabling the citizens to have recourse to a convenient and effective forum for determination of complaints and thereby save him from pursuing his remedy through the process of Courts, which may prove to be expensive or dilatory and may not facilitate speedy determination.

4. The concept of having an institution like the Lokpal arises from the need for redressal of citizens' grievances. The term Lokpal is akin to the English term 'Ombudsman' which has been described in Chamber's Dictionary as a 'grievance man'. Ombudsman means an official who is appointed to investigate complaints against the administration. In other words, Ombudsman is an officer who investigates complaints of citizens of unfair treatment meted out to them by Government Departments and suggests remedy thereof, if he finds that a complaint is justified. The

institution of Ombudsman came into being in 1713 in Sweden when Chancellor of justice was appointed by the King to act as an invigilator to look into the functioning of the war time Government. In the year 1809, provision was made for the appointment of Ombudsman by the legislature. The institution remained mainly confined to the Scandinavian countries such as Finland and Denmark. In 1962 New Zealand also adopted the system of Ombudsman. Great Britain also did not lag behind and a slightly modified version of the institution in the form of the office of Parliamentary Commissioner came into being through an Act of Parliament in 1967. This was followed by other countries such as Canada, Australia, U.S.A. France and several newly independent countries of Africa and Asia.

5. A study of the system of Ombudsman or similar institutions in Sweden, United Kingdom, Zambia and Nigeria brings into focus the fact that mainly complaints of mal-administration are looked into by the Ombudsman there and Ministers etc. do not seem to have been brought within their purview. However, in Denmark all administrative matters concerning all units of State administration including Ministers and in Norway administrative aspects of acts of Ministers have been brought within the purview of Ombudsman. In Tanzania and Uganda the areas of jurisdiction for the institutions which are known as Anti Corruption Squad and Inspector General of Government, respectively, are mainly targetted at corruption and abuse of public office. The thrust of the system of Ombudsman as obtaining in these countries is mainly on redressal of public grievances arising mainly out of their complaints of mal-administration.

6. In so far as India is concerned animated discussions both inside Parliament as well as outside took place preceding examination of the issue by the Administrative Reforms Commission on the need for setting up an Ombudsman like institution to investigate and report on complaints pertaining to corruption. Coupled with this was the felt necessity for the establishment of an independent authority for the redressal of public grievances. The idea, however, could not be formalised till the Administrative Reforms Commission in its interim Report submitted in 1966 suggested that:

"The special circumstances relating to our country can be fully met by providing for two special institutions for the redress of citizens' grievances. There should be one authority dealing with complaints against the administrative acts of Ministers or Secretaries to Government at the Centre and in the States. There should be another authority in each State and at the Centre and for dealing with complaints against the administrative acts of other officials... The setting up of these authorities should not, however, be taken to be a complete answer to the problem of redress of citizens' grievances. They only provide the ultimate set-up for such redress as has not been available through the normal departmental or governmental machinery and do not absolve the department from fulfilling its obligations to the citizen for administering its affairs without generating, as far as possible, any legitimate sense of grievance. Thus, the administration itself must play the major role in reducing the area of grievances and providing remedies wherever necessary and feasible... When this machinery (in-built departmental machinery) functions effectively, the number of cases which will have to go to an authority outside the Ministry or the Department should be comparatively small in number."

7. The Administrative Reforms Commission thus contemplated a very limited role of the proposed creation of an institution like the Lokpal which would only inquire into complaints against a specified category of persons and not be a forum to deal with all complaints of citizens' grievances. As the Administrative Reforms Commission itself emphasised that 'the responsibility of the Departments to deal adequately with public grievances must squarely be faced by them', the institution of Lokpal was thought of something in the nature of a set up for redress as has not been available through the normal departmental or governmental machinery. The Administrative Reforms Commission also underscored an important point when it referred to the special circumstances relating to our country's vastness and enormous size of population which would virtually make it quite stupendous, if not impossible, for a single agency to deal with the vast magnitude of complaints of public grievances and provide a remedy therefor. The proposed Lokpal Bill, therefore, has mainly been devised to provide a forum to the citizens to make complaints of corruption against public functionaries who have been defined to mean persons who hold or have held the office of the Prime Minister, Minister of State or Deputy Minister of the Union and are or have been Members of either House of Parliament.

8. The Committee held twelve sittings in all to consider and finalise its report on this Bill.

9. In its first sitting held on October 8, 1996 the Committee discussed the Bill in general and having regard to the special importance of the Bill which sought to establish an institution of this kind at the national level, the Committee decides to invite memoranda from the individuals/organisations/institutions' etc. interested in the subject matter of the Bill. The Committee also decided to issue a Press communique in this behalf fixing November 18, 1996 as the last date for the receipt of memoranda. On the 10th October, 1996, the Director General, Doordarshan and All India Radio were also requested to telecast/broadcast the matter repeatedly to give it wide publicity so as to elicit public opinion on the Bill.

10. In all 110 memoranda containing comments and suggestions on the provisions of the Bill were received by the Committee from various organisations, associations and individuals etc. At its sitting held on

February 6, 1997 the Committee heard the Secretary of the administrative Ministry concerned with the Bill, namely the Ministry of Personnel, Public Grievances and Pensions on the Bill. At its sittings held on the 19th February and 3rd, 4th,17th, 18th, 19th and 20th March, 1997, the Committee heard the viewsof some former bureaucrats, journalists and representatives of various political parties and institutions and organisations on the subject The Committee wishes to express its thanks to all the persons who either appeared before it or sent their valuable suggestions/ views on the provisions of the Bill for the benefit of the Committee.

11. The Committee considered various papers and memoranda placed before it and also the views expressed by the witnesses on the Bill.

12. At its sittings held on the 29th April and 1st May, 1997 the Committee took up clause-by-clause consideration of the Bill.

13. The Committee considered and adopted the Report at its sitting held on the 6th May, 1997.

14. The observations of the Committee with regard to the principal changes proposed in the Bill are given below:-

Clause 3

The Committee is of the view that sub-clause (b) of clause 3 (2) be substituted to read as follows:-

"two Members who are, or have been, judges of the Supreme Court or the Chief Justice of the High Courts"

Clause 4

The Committee notes that the seven Member Committee, which has been proposed for recommending the names for appointment as Chairman and Members of the Lokpal, seems to be heavily loaded in favour of the party/parties in Government, giving excessive leverage to the ruling party/ combine in the appointment process, and as such it would not inspire public confidence. The Committee is, therefore, of the view that the first proviso to clause 4(1) be substituted to read as follows:-

Provided that every appointment under this sub-section shall be made after obtaining the recommendations of a Committee consisting of -

a) the Vice President of India - Chairman;
b) the Prime Minister - Member;
c) Speaker of the House of the People - Member;
d) Leader of the Opposition in the House of the People - Member;
e) Leader of the Opposition in the Council of States - Member.

Clause 6

The Members of the Lokpal have been ensured a fixed tenure of 5 years. The Committee feels that no mechanism has been envisaged in the Bill to evaluate the performance of the Lokpal and in that context the fixed tenure of 5 years appears to be rather too long. Besides, in case the retired Chief Justice or judges of the Supreme Court are appointed as the Chairman/ Members of the Lokpal well past the age of 65 years, their continuance upto the age of 70 years would perhaps be a factor to reckon with. The Committee, therefore, recommends that the term of office of the Members of the Lokpal be reduced to 3 years and Clause 6 be amended accordingly.

Clause 7

The Committee has noted that under this Clause a Member of the Lokpal can be removed from his office only by an order made by the President on the ground of proved misbehaviour of incapacity after an inquiry made by the Chief Justice of India or as the case may be, by such other judge of the Supreme Court as the Chief Justice of India may nominate in this behalf. Clause 3(2) (a) stipulates that the Chairman of the Lokpal shall be a person who is or has been a Chief Justice or judge of the Supreme Court. Similarly, Cluase 3(2) (b) prescribes that the members of the Lokpal shall be persons who are or have been or are qualified to be a judge of the Supreme Court (recommended by the Committee to be amended). The existing procedure for removal of judges of the Supreme Court and the High Courts as laid down under Articles 124 (4) and (5) read with Article 218 of the Constitution is by an order of the President on an Address being presented to him by requisite number of members of each House of Parliament. The Committee feels that the status of Chairman and the members of the Lokpal as envisaged under the scheme of the BIll is skin to the Chief Justice/judges of the Supreme Court and hence the procedure for their removal should be more stringent if not analogous to the one as laid down in the Constitution. The Committee, accordingly, is of the view that the inquiry against a member of the Lokpal as contemplated under Cause 7 for his removal should be made by the Chief Justice of India and the two senior most judges of the Supreme Court. Clause 7 may be amended accordingly.

Clause 8

The Committee has noted that the Lokpal has *inter-alia* been empowered *vide* Clause 8(2) (i) to secure the services of any officer or employee or investigating agency of the Central Government or the State Government with the concurrence of that Government for the purpose of dealing with any complaints or any classes of complaints. Similarly, it has been ensured *vide* Clause 8(2) (ii) that the Lokpal does not suffer in any way in the investigation of the Complaints made to it and for that purpose, if need be, it can secure the services of any other person or agency which implies even private persons or agencies. The Committee expressed the apprehension that the provision relating to seeking the concurrence of concerned Governments for securing services of any officer may delay the investigation. Hence the Committee is of the view that in order to remove any apprehensions on this score, steps may be taken to ensure that the services of officers, etc. to the Lokpal are provided with due promptness and necessary procedure in this regard may be provided in the rules to be framed under this Act.

Clause 9

The Committee feels that the amplitude of the discretionary power vested in the Lokpal under Clause 9(1) by the usage of the words 'the Lokpal may' is far too large. The Committee is accordingly of the view that subject to the other provisions of this Act the Lokpal should be under a mandatory obligation to inquire into the subject matter of the complaint. The word "may" in sub-clause (1) of this clause may be substituted by the word "shall". The Committee also feels that when the complaints about allegations of corruption against public functionaries are sought to be brought within the purview of the Lokpal, there is no reason for such complaints being taken up at any other forum such as the Commissions of Inquiry. The Committee is, therefore, of the opinion that the amount of discretion conferred on the Lokpal *vide* sub-clause (3) of clause 9 in the matter of referring any complaint for inquiry under the Commissions of Inquiry Act, 1952, is not desirable and the words 'except on the recommendation, or with the concurrence, of the Lokpal' occuring therein be deleted. Clause 9 may be amended accordingly.

Clause 10

In view of the recommendation made by the Committee for omitting the discretionary aspect of Lokpal from sub-clause (3) of clause 9, sub-clause (2) of clause 10 becomes redundant and hence it may be deleted.

In terms of sub clause (3) of clause 10, the jurisdiction of Lokpal is restricted to inquiring into complaints in respect of offences which are alleged to have been committed during the previous five years. The Committee has, however noted that some time information about corruption cases of immense proportions surfaces very late and national interest demands that truth must come out and the guilty be brought to book. Besides, the Committee is given to understand that in some of the Lok Ayukta Acts in force in some of the

States, the provision exists for inquiry into complaints in respect of offences alleged to have been committed upto ten years earlier. The Committee, therefore,is of the opinion that the period of five years occuring in sub-clause (3) of clause 10 be substituted to read as ten years.

Clause 11

The Committee has noted that under sub-clause (3) of clause 11, it is enjoined upon the complaint to make a deposit of a sum of rupees one thousand but the manner of making this deposit and the authority or agency with which the deposit is to be made are left to be prescribed in the rules to be framed under clause 32. The Committee is of the opinion that if a fixed amount is prescribed in thé Act itself, the concerned authority will have to come before Parliament every time they wish to enhance/modify the fee which very often becomes essential because of the changing value of money. Hence, the Committee is of the opinion that this can be taken care of in the rules. The Committee feels, that this provision should be amended accordingly.

Clause 12

In view of the change proposed by the Committee in sub-clause (3) of clause 10 for raising the period of limitation for complaints from 5 years to 10 years, consequential change should be made in clause 12 (1) (a) and the period of 5 years mentioned therein be substituted to read as 10 years. Likewise, since the Committee has recommended deletion of sub-clause (2) of clause 10 consequential change in clause 12 (1) (b) should also be effected.

The Committee is of the view that the wording of sub-clauses (c) and (d) of clause 12 (1) confers unguided and arbitrary powers of *in-limine* rejection of complaints on the Lokpal. It is in public interest that the complaints should be properly investigated and disposed of rather than nipped in the bud. Sub-clause (1) (c) should accordingly be reworded to read 'that the complaint is manifestly false and vexatious' and sub-clause (1) (d) should be deleted in toto.

Clause 13

Sub-clause (2) of clause 13 stipulates that every inquiry shall be conducted *in camera* by the Chairman and the Members of the Lokpal sitting jointly. The Committee feels that this is not in consonance with the system of open court hearings currently prevalent in our country. One of the essential ingredients of democratic functioning of Government is increased participation of people in the governance of the country and their right to information. The very nature of conducting proceedings or trials by the judicial or quasi-judicial organs in camera leads one to believe that truth is being shrouded in mystery. The Committee, therefore, feels that people of the country have a right to know about the acts of the public functionaries and accordingly they should have access to the inquiries being conducted by the Lokpal. The Committee, therefore, recommends that sub-clause (2) of clause 13 be amended and the words *in camera* be substituted by the words in open and a proviso be added thereto as follows:

"Provided that the Chairman and the Members of the Lokpal may conduct an inquiry *in camera* in exceptional circumstances for reasons to be recorded in writing."

Clause 14

The Committee has noted that by the powers conferred under clause 14, the Lokpal can stop investigations being pursued by the Police Officials under the Code of Criminal Procedure, 1973, solely on the ground that such investigations might prejudicially affect the conduct of inquiry in respect of complaints made to it. The Committee feels that it will not be proper to allow the Lokpal, whose jurisdiction is restricted to making inquiry into allegations of corruption, to hamper investigations being conducted under the normal criminal law of the country. The Committee is accordingly of the opinion that clause 14 be omitted from the Bill.

Clause 15

The Committee has noted that under sub-clause (4) of clause 15, information as may be relevant or useful to the conduct of an inquiry by the Lokpal can be withheld on various grounds as mentioned thereunder so much so that the Secretary to the Government of India or Chief Secretary of the State Government have been given extensive powers to refuse to make available necessary information to the Lokpal. The Committee is of the opinion that sub-clause (4) is inconsistent with the nature of the proceedings before the Lokpal. Denial of such information will reduce the institution of Lokpal to a mockery and will create doubts in the public mind. Therefore, sub-clause (4) of clause 15 should be deleted. In view of this recommendation of the Committee, sub-clause (3) of clause 15 should also be consequentially amended.

Clause 16

The Committee feels that the powers conferred on the Lokpal under the provisions of clause 16(1) and (2) for purposes of search and seizure of documents, which may be useful for or relevant to any inquiry being conducted by it, are quite adequate. The proviso may, however, be modified to read as follows:

"Provided that in cases where such documents are required to be returned, the Lokpal shall return the documents after retaining.copies thereof with due authentication."

The Explanation added after the proviso appears to be unnecessary to the Committee and hence it should be deleted.

Clause 17

The Committee has noted that sub-clause (a) of clause (17) (1) confers power on the Lokpal to close the cases in the event of the allegations made in the complaint not being substantiated either wholly or partly. Sub-clause (b) of clause 17(1), on the other hand, enjoins upon it to make a Report in writing to the competent authority in case all or any of the allegations made in the complaint have or has been substantiated either wholly or partly. The Committee feels that after inquiry, whether the offences alleged in the complaint are found to have been substantiated or not, either wholly or partly it should be incumbent upon the Lokpal to make a Report of its findings to the competent authority and intimate the complainant and the public functionary about its having made the Report.

The Committee is also of the view that the Lokpal should, while communicating its findings and recommendations in its Report to the competent authority, clearly specify the action to be taken against the public functionary against whom the offence alleged in the complaint has been found to be substantiated, either wholly or partly. Rather, the functioning of the Lokpal should be made more transparent and its pronouncements should be made public and under no circumstances, it should be empowered to record a finding, closing the case which can at best be confined to stating that, upon inquiry the offences alleged in the complaint have not been substantiated, either wholly or partly. In this manner the public functionary would get due justice. The Committee, accordingly, recommends that sub-clauses (a) and (b) of clause 17(1) may be combined into one clause to read as follows:-

"At the conclusion of the inquiry, the Lokpal shall determine whether all or any of the offences alleged in the complaints have or has been proved to its satisfaction. The Lokpal shall report its findings to the complaint, the public functionary and the competent authority."

Consequential amendment in this clause be made accordingly to re-number it as 17(1) instead of 17(1)(a) and (b).

The Committee has noted that in terms of sub-clause 17(2), the examination of a Report in respect of Prime Minister received from the Lokpal by the competent authority and communication of a decision thereon to the Lokpal within the prescribed period seems to have been precluded.

The matter is left *vide* sub-clause (3) of clause 17 to the discretion of the House of the People or the Council of States to which the Prime Minister belongs merely by the laying of the Report. The Committee feels that the Act has to be uniformly applicable to all the public functionaries including the Prime Minister and accordingly recommends that the words "other than the Prime Minister" occurring in sub-clause (2) of clause 17 should be deleted. The Committee is also of the opinion that the period of 90 days prescribed under sub-clause (3) for laying of the Report of the Lokpal before the House of the People or the Council of States, as the case may be, read with the Explanation appended thereto, is quite unreasonable and it should be omitted from the clause along with the Explanation. Instead sub-clause (3) may be amended to provide for laying of the Report after its receipt before the House of the people or the Council of States, as the case may be, within the first week on their assembling for a Session. The Committee feels that since sub-clause (3) of clause 17 relates to the laying of Reports in respect of complaints against public functionaries received from the Lokpal, it should have precedence for chronological reasons over sub-clause (2) and accordingly, sub-clause (3), as amended, be re-numbered as sub-clause (2) and sub-clause (2) be re-numbered as sub-clause (3).

Clause 18

In the view of the committee, clause-18 which provides for declaration of assets by the Members of Parliament, before the Lokpal every year, should be amended to provide for furnishing of return by the members within a period of 90 days on their becoming members and annually thereafter, within 90 days of commencement of each Financial Year. An explanation should also be added to the clause to define the family as including both the spouse and dependent children.

The Committee has also noted that clause-18 is too general in nature and does not refer to the consequences as may flow in case the members of Parliament either do not furnish a return of assets to the Lokpal or furnish incomplete or false return. The Committee accordingly recommends that a provision be made in the Bill to include, that the details of the returns filed by the Members of Parliament will be reported by the Lokpal to the Chairpersons of the House of the People and the Council of States. A deterrent clause may also be inserted to deal with cases of non-filing or delayed filing of returns by the Members of Parliament or their filing them in an incomplete or falsified manner.

Clause 19

The Committee feels that the language of clause-19 be slightly modified in the interest of clarity to substitute the words "the Members" with the words "the Chairman and the Members of the Lokpal".

Clause 20

This clause provides for secrecy of information and evidence collected during any inquiry by the Lokpal. Even courts also cannot have any access to this evidence. The Committee feels that this clause negates the concept of transparency in the functioning of the institution of Lokpal. There is no denying the fact that the evidence collected by the Lokpal will be at tremendous cost of men and material and keeping in view the fact that Lokpal under the proposed scheme of the Bill will not be the prosecuting or punishing authority against public functionaries held guilty, the bar placed on the use of evidence by the courts is not justified. On the contrary, allowing the Courts to have access to the evidence or information collected by the Lokpal will save them considerable time and botheration. Taking a view in its totality about clause 20, the Committee holds that as it is too secretive and bars flow of information, it should be deleted.

Clause 21

The Committee is in broad agreement with the provisions of clause 21 as the dignity of the office of the Lokpal is to be respected and protected. The Committee, however, is of the view that sub-clause (2) of Clause 21 is too wide in its language and may well be an unreasonable restriction on free speech. Besides, the purpose contemplated under sub-clause (2) is by and large achieved by sub-clause (1) and (3) and hence there does not appear to be any need to retain sub-clause (2). Hence, it should be deleted. Consequentially, the reference to sub-clause (2) in sub-clause (3) be deleted.

Clause 22

This clause seeks to confer powers on the Lokpal to try certain offences summarily and punish the persons who tender false evidence before it. The Committee however, feels that provisions for summary trails for offences of this nature already exist in the Code of Criminal Procedure, 1973 and there does not appear to be any need to specifically provide sub-clause (1) for this purpose. Hence, it should be deleted. Likewise, the Committee feels that in sub-clause (2) of clause 22 reference to sections 175, 178, 179 and 180 of the Indian Penal Code is unnecessary and the words occurring therein from "in Section 175, ... to the Indian Penal Code" be substituted by the words "in clause 21(1) of this Act".

The Committee has noted that under sub-clause (4) of clause 22 an appeal has been allowed to be made to the High Court by persons convicted under clause 22 by the Lokpal. This, however, does not appear to be proper as the status of the Chairman and Members of the Lokpal is equivalent to the status of the Chief Justice and Judges of the Supreme Court and accordingly, an appeal against the conviction pronounced by the Lokpal should lie to the Supreme Court and not to the High Court. The Committee, therefore, recommends that sub-clause (4) may be amended to provide for appeals to the Supreme Court and the Explanation to this clause which consequently becomes redundant should also be deleted.

Clause 23, 24 and 25

Clause 23 makes printing or publication of any information in relation to any complaint before the inquiry under the Act has reached its definitive stage, an offence triable summarily by the Lokpal. The ground on which this is based is that disclosure of information in such a manner causes irreparable damage to the public functionaries, particularly, in cases where the public functionary has been absolved of the charges against him. Similarly clause 24 provides for the punishment which may be awarded by the Lokpal to a person making a complaint which is found by the Lokpal to be false. In cases, both under clauses 23 and 24 provision for appeal against sentence of conviction pronounced by the Lokpal has been made to the Supreme Court. Clause 25 has been provided for the modified application of the provisions of the Code of Criminal Procedure for the trial of offences under clause 22, 23 and 24.

The Committee has already recommended holding of inquiries by the Lokpal in the open, save in exceptional circumstances for reasons to be recorded in writing for in camera proceedings. The Committee has also stressed that there has to be transparency in the functioning of the Lokpal. Clause 23 on the contrary, seems to put unnecessary fetters on the right of expression and freedom of speech of the people by making the proceedings of the Lokpal too secretive and conferring extensive powers on it to punish the person who may be adjudged guilty. Similarly, clause 24 is too severe. The Committee feels that the Lokpal should not convert itself into a criminal court except for the purposes of punishing *ex-facie* cases of contempt under clause 21(1). It sounds logical that if the Lokpal has no power to punish a guilty public functionary, he should have no power to prosecute and punish the complainant or any witness. Such persons may be left to be prosecuted under the Indian Penal Code in the normal course. Therefore, in view of the recommendation of the Committee for open inquiry by the Lokpal and the fact that the sweep of the penal provisions under clauses 23 and 24 is too wide, the Committee recommends that clauses 23 and 24 may be dropped. As the Committee has recommended dropping of clauses 23 and 24, clause 25 consequentially becomes redundant and it may also be dropped.

Clause 26

Clause 26 places a bar on prosecution in respect of allegations not proved or not substantiated before the Lokpal. This clause appears to be too draconian in nature and substance as it makes the Lokpal or the competent authority the final arbiters in determining the complaints of corruption against public functionaries. It is well known that even under the ordinary law of the land appeals have been provided at various stages in the courts and here, under this clause, the complaints who may not be satisfied with the decision of the Lokpal have been left high and dry as they cannot approach any court against the decision of the Lokpal or the competent authority. The Committee, therefore, feels that this clause in not in consonance with the judicial system of a democratic polity and it may be dropped altogether. It should be left to the complainants to approach the courts against the decision of the Lokpal/competent authority to seek appropriate remedies.

Clause 27

Clause 27 requires the Lokpal to inquire into any allegation as may be the subject matter of a complaint under this Act on an order being issued by the President and subject to such conditions or limitations as may be specified therein notwithstanding anything contained in the Act. The implication of the wording of this clause is perhaps that the only limitation of this Act which applies to the order issued by the President is that the allegation which is referred to the Lokpal for inquiry has to be only in respect of which a complaint may be made and no other provisions of the Act seem to apply while determining the truthfulness or otherwise of the allegation. It may perhaps be that the allegation cited in the complaint may relate to a matter more than 10 years old. The Committee is, therefore, of the view that the words "notwithstanding anything contained in this Act" occurring in clause 27 be substituted by the words "subject to the provisions of clause 12".

Clauses 28 and 29

Clause 28 provides for the disposal of deposits made by the complainants and clause 29 provides for compensation or reward or both, payable to complainant in the event of all or any of the allegations made in a complaint being substantiated. The Committee feels that the areas covered by clauses 28 and 29 are somewhat inter-linked and it will be more appropriate if both these clauses are combined into one and provision is made for the amount of compensation/reward or punishment to be decided by the Lokpal while concluding its findings. The Committee is also of the view that the words occurring at the end of clause 29 (which may be combined with clause 28 in appropriate form) *viz.* "and the Central Government shall pay, the amount or amounts so determined, to the complainant" be substituted by the words "and the Lokpal shall determine the person by whom the said compensation or award shall be paid after giving that person a reasonable opportunity of being heard".

Clause 30

The Committee has noted that sub-clause (2) of clause 30 bars court's jurisdiction on the proceedings or decisions of the Lokpal. The Committee understands that the Supreme Court under Article 32 and the High Court under Article 226 of the Constitution have inherent writ jurisdiction and aggrieved citizens can always approach these courts in matters where their rights have been encroached upon. Viewed in that context and in view of the fact that the Committee has already recommended deletion of clause 26, sub-clause (2) of clause 30 may be dropped.

Clause 31

The Committee feels that in view of the recommendation made by it for dropping sub-clause (1) of clause 22 and clauses 23 and 24, consequential changes may be made in clause 31.

Clause 33

Sub-clause (b) of clause 33 bars any inquiry *suo-motu* by the Lokpal into cases of corruption by public functionaries coming to his notice through media or otherwise. The Committee feels that the basic objective of the creation of an institution of Lokpal is to cleanse public life from the scourge of corruption and, therefore, the Lokpal should not be fettered in being barred from jurisdiction to make inquiry upon its own knowledge and information. It should be given powers to take *suo-motu* notice of cases of corruption by public functionaries and accordingly sub-clause (b) of clause 33 may be deleted.

Clause 35

The Committee feels that clause 35 be suitably amended to take care of the amendment suggested by it in sub-clause (3) of clause 9.

Clause 1, the Enacting Formula and the Title

The Committee is of the view that the consequential changes in respect of Clause 1, the Enacting Formula and the Title with reference to the year of enactment as indicated therein may also be carried out.

15. The Committee agrees with the provisions contained in the remaining clauses of the Bill.

16. In view of the above recommendations/observations some necessary changes of consequential or drafting nature may also have to be carried out in the Bill and some of the clauses may also have to be renumbered.

17. The Committee recommends that the Bill be passed after incorporating the amendments suggested by it.

SOM PAL
Chairman,
Committee on Home Affairs

NEW DELHI;
May 6, 1997

ANNEXURE 3

DRAFT LOKPAL BILL, 1966

As proposed by the Administrative Reforms Commission vide their Interim Report on "Problems of Citizens' grievances" submitted to Prime Minister on 20 October, 1966.

A BILL to make provision for the appointment and functions of an authority named Lokpal for the investigation of administrative acts in certain cases and for matters connected therewith.

Be it enacted by Parliament in the seventeenth year of the Republic of India as follows:

CHAPTER I

PRELIMINARY

Short title, extend and commencement.

1. (1) This Act may be called the Lokpal Act, 1966.
   (2) It extends to the whole of India.
   (3) It shall come into force on such day as the Central Government may, be notification in the Official Gazette, appoint.

Definitions.

2. In this Act,
   "action" includes failure to act.
   "Minister" means a person appointed to be a member of the Council of Ministers whether of the Union or of a State and by whatever name called.
   "Secretary" means a person appointed to be Secretary to the Government of India or a State Government.

CHAPTER II

THE LOKPAL

3. (1) The President shall, on the advice of the Prime Minister, appoint a person to be known as the Lokpal for exercising the powers and performing the functions assigned to the Lokpal under this Act.

(2) The Prime Minister shall tender the advice to the President, referred to in sub-section (1), after consultation with the Chief Justice of India and the Leader of the Opposition in the Lok Sabha, or, if there be no such leader, a person elected for the purpose of this sub-section by the member of the Opposition in the Lok Sabha, in such manner as the Speaker may direct.

(3) Before he enters upon his office, the person appointed as Lokpal shall

(a) if he be a Member of Parliament or of the Legislature of any State, resign his membership of Parliament or of the Legislature, as the case may be;

(b) if he be the holder of any office of profit, resign from such office;

(c) if he be connected with any business, sever his connection with that business.

(d) if he be connected with any political party, sever his connection with that party.

Conditions of Service

4. (1) Every person appointed as Lokpal shall hold office for a term of five years from the date on which he enters upon his office but shall be eligible for re-appointment for one more term.

(2) Notwithstanding anything contained in sub-section(1), the Lokpal may:

(a) by writing under his hand addressed to the President, resign his office at any time,

(b) be removed from his office in accordance with the provisions of sub-section (3).

(3) The Lokpal shall not be removed from his office except by an order of the President passed after an address by each House of Parliament supported by a majority of the total membership of that House and by a majority of not less than two-thirds of the members of that House present and voting has been presented to the President in the same session for such removal on the ground of proved misbehavior or incapacity.

(4) The law, if any, passed by Parliament for regulating the procedure for the presentation of an address and for the investigation and proof of the misbehavior or incapacity of a Judge under clause (5) of

Article 124 of the Constitution will also apply mutatis mutandis to the Lokpal.

(5) On ceasing to hold office, the Lokpal shall be ineligible for further employment either under the Government of India or under the Government of a State or any Government Undertaking.

(6) The Lokpal shall have the same status, salary and allowances and conditions of service as the Chief Justice of India.

Oath of office.

5. Every person appointed as Lokpal shall, before he enters upon his office, make and subscribe before the person prescribed by the President in that behalf, an oath according to the form set out hereunder.

I, A.B. "having been appointed a Lokpal do swear in the name of God/solemnly affirm that I will bear true faith and allegiance to the Constitution of India as by law established and I will duly and faithfully and to the best of my ability, knowledge, and judgment perform the duties of my office without fear or favour, affection or ill-will."

6. (1) The Lokpal may appoint such officers and employees as may be necessary for the efficient discharge of his functions under this Act. Provided that the category of officers and employees and the number thereof that may be appointed under this section shall from time to time be fixed with the approval of the President.

(2) The salaries of persons appointed under this section and their conditions of service shall be such as are approved by the President.

CHAPTER III

FUNCTIONS AND POWERS OF THE LOKPAL

Matters subject to his investigation.

7. (1) Subject to the provisions of this Act, the Lokpal may investigate any action taken by or with the approval of a Minister of Secretary, being action taken in the exercise of his administrative functions, in any case where :

(a) a written complaint is duly made to the Lokpal by a person (i) who claims to have sustained injustice in consequence of maladministration in connection with such action, or (ii) who affirms that such action has resulted in favour being unduly shown to any person or in accrual of personal benefit or gain to the Minister or to the Secretary, as the case may be, or

(b) information has come to his knowledge otherwise than on a complaint under clause (a) that such action is of the nature mentioned in that clause.

(2) Except as hereinafter provided, the Lokpal shall not conduct an investigation under this Act in respect of any of the following matters, that is to say,

(a) any action in respect of which the person aggrieved has or had a right of appeal, reference, or review to or before a tribunal constituted by or under any enactment;

(b) any action in respect of which the person aggrieved has or had a remedy by way of proceedings in any court of law.

Provided that the Lokpal may conduct an investigation notwithstanding that the person aggrieved has or had a remedy by way of proceedings in a court of law if he is satisfied that in the particular circumstances it is not reasonable to expect him to take or to have taken such proceedings.

(3) A complaint shall not be entertained under this Act unless it is made not later than twelve months from the date on which action complained against took place.

(4) The Lokpal may in his discretion refuse to investigate or may cease to investigate an administrative action if he is satisfied that

(a) a remedy for the injustice alleged to have been caused thereby exists and he is of the opinion that the complainant should seek his remedy accordingly, or

(b) the complaint against the action is trivial, frivolous, or is not made in good faith, or

(c) there are no sufficient grounds for proceeding with his investigations.

(5) In any case where the Lokpal decides that he will not investigate or that he will cease to investigate an administrative action complained of or that the complainant should seek his remedy elsewhere, he shall inform the complainant accordingly.

(6) Without prejudice to sub-section (2) of this section, the Lokpal shall not conduct an investigation under this Act in respect of any of the following matters:

(a) Action taken in a matter certified by a Union Minister as affecting the relations or dealings between the Government of India and any foreign Government or any international organisation of States or Governments.

(b) Action taken under the Extradition Act, 1962 or the Foreigners' Act, 1946.

(c) Action taken for the purpose of investigating crime or protecting the security of the State including action taken with respect to passports.

(d) Action taken in the exercise of power in relation to determining whether a matter shall go to a court or not.

(e) Action taken in matters which arise out of the terms of contract governing purely commercial relations of the administration with customers or suppliers, except where the complainant alleges harassment or gross delay in meeting contractual obligations.

(f) Action taken in respect of appointments, removals, pay, discipline, superannuation or other personnel matters.

(g) Grant of honours and awards.

(h) A decision made in exercise of his discretion by an administrative authority unless the elements involved in the exercise of discretion are absent to such an extent that no discretion has been exercised at all.

Procedure in respect of investigations.

8. (1) Where the Lokpal proposes to conduct an investigation under this Act, he shall afford the Minister or Secretary concerned an opportunity to comment on any allegations of maladministration made against such Minister or Secretary.

(2) Every such investigation shall be conducted in private except as aforesaid the procedure for conducting an investigation shall be such as the Lokpal considers appropriate in the circumstances of the case.

Evidence.

9. (1) Subject to the provisions of this section, for the purposes of investigation under this Act, the Lokpal may require any Minister or officer or any other person who in his opinion is able to furnish information or produce documents relevant to the investigation to furnish any such information or produce any such document.

(2) For the purpose of any such investigation the Lokpal shall have all the powers of a Civil Court while trying the suit under the Code of Civil Procedure, 1908 in respect of the following matters.

(a) summoning and enforcing the attendance of any person and examining him on oath,

(b) discovery and production of documents

(c) receiving evidence on affidavits,

(d) receiving any public record or copy thereof from any office.

(3) Subject to the provisions of sub-section (4) of this section, no obligation to maintain secrecy or other restriction upon the disclosure of information obtained by or furnished to Government or persons in Government service, whether impose by any enactment or by any rule of law, shall apply to the disclosure of information for the purposes of investigation under this Act.

(4) No person shall be required or authorised by virtue of this Act to furnish any information or answer any question or produce any document:

(a) which might prejudice the security or defence or international relations of India (including India's relations with the Government of any other country or with any international organisation), or the investigation or detection of crime, or

(b) which might involve the disclosure of proceedings of the Cabinet or any Committee of the Cabinet, and for the purposes of this sub-section a certificate issued by the Secretary of the Cabinet of the Central Government of the Chief Secretary of the State concerned with the approval of the Prime Minister or the Chief Minister of the State, as the case may be, certifying that any information, question or document is of such a nature, shall be conclusive.

(5) For the purpose of enforcing the attendance of witnesses, the legal limits of the Lokpal's jurisdiction shall be the limits of the territory of India.

(6) Subject to the provisions of sub-section (3) of this section, no person shall be compelled for the purposes of investigation under this Act to give any evidence or produce any document which he could not be compelled to give or produce in proceedings before a Court.

Obstruction and Contempt

10. (1) If any person without lawful excuse obstructs the Lokpal in the performance of his functions under this Act or is guilty of any act or omission in relation to an investigation under this Act which, if that investigation were a proceeding before a court, would constitute contempt of court, the Lokpal may certify the offence to the Supreme Court. For this purpose, if in connection with a complaint made under para (ii) of clause (a) of sub-section (1) of section 7, a person makes a false statement before the Lokpal knowing it to be false he shall be deemed to be guilty of an act constituting contempt of court.

(2) Where an offence is certified under this section, the Supreme Court may inquire into the matter and dispose it of as if it related to a charge of contempt of the Supreme Court itself.

Reports by the Lokpal

11. (1) After taking into consideration the comments of the Minister or the Secretary, as the case may be, the Lokpal may decide not to proceed further with the investigation in which case he will inform the complainant accordingly.

(2) In any case where the Lokpal decides further to conduct an investigation under this Act, he shall send an intimation of the same to the Minister or the Secretary concerned and the complainant.

(3) If after conducting an investigation under this Act, it appears to the Lokpal that injustice has been caused to the person aggrieved

in consequence of maladministration, he shall inform the Minister or Secretary concerned, as the case may be, and require that it be remedied within such period as he may in his discretion and having regard to the circumstances of the case deem sufficient.

(4) If the injustice is not remedied or the Lokpal considers that it will not be remedied he may bring the matter to the notice of the Prime Minister or the Chief Minister of the State, as the case may be, who will intimate to the Lokpal the action taken in the matter within a period of two months.

(5) If the Lokpal is satisfied with the action taken he will close the case but where he is not so satisfied and he considers that the case so deserves, he may make a special report upon the case to the Lok Sabha or the legislative assembly of the State concerned, as the case may be.

(6) If as a result of his investigation the Lokpal comes to the conclusion that the administrative action of a Minister or Secretary has resulted in a favour being unduly shown to any person or in the accrual of a personal benefit or gain to the Minister or the Secretary, as the case may be, he shall communicate his conclusion along with the material on the basis of which he has arrived at the conclusion to the Prime Minister or the Chief Minister concerned. The Prime Minister or the Chief Minister concerned shall thereupon take such action as is considered necessary on the report and information the Lokpal within two months of the receipt thereof of the action taken or proposed to be taken thereon.

(7) The Lokpal shall lay before the Parliament or the legislature of the State concerned annual reports on the performance of his functions under this Act.

12. (1) It is hereby declared that the Lokpal, his officers and other employees are subject to the provisions of the Official Secrets Act.

(2) Information obtained by the Lokpal or his officers in the course of or for purposes of investigation under this Act shall not be disclosed except :

(a) For purposes of the investigation and for any report to be made thereon under this Act ;

(b) For purposes of any proceedings for an offence under the Official Secrets Act or an offence of prejury or for purposes of any proceedings under Section 10 of this Act.

(3) The Lokpal and his officers shall not be called upon to give any evidence in any proceedings (other than such proceedings as aforesaid) of matters coming to his or their knowledge in the course of an investigation under this Act.

(4) A minister may give notice in writing to the Lokpal with respect

to any documents or information specified in the notice or any class of documents so specified that in the opinion of the Minister the disclosure of the documents or information of that class would be contrary to the public interests and where such a notice is given, nothing in this Act shall be construed as authorising or requiring the Lokpal or any officer of the Lokpal to communicate to any person any document or information specified in the notice or any document or information of a class so specified.

(5) No person shall publish any proceedings relating to an investigation which is pending before the Lokpal ; nor shall any person publish such proceedings after the investigation is completed unless prior permission for the publication is obtained from the Lokpal.

(6) Any person committing a breach of sub-section (5) of this section shall be treated as having committed contempt for the purposes of section 10 and on any such contempt being certified by the Lokpal, the Supreme Court shall deal with it as if it were a case of contempt before that court.

(7) Nothing in sub-sections (5) and (6) shall apply to the publication of any report sent by the Lokpal to the complainant or to the Lok Sabha or to the Legislature of a State as the case may be.

Protection of Action taken in Good Faith

13. No suit, prosecution, or other proceeding shall lie against the Lokpal or any of his officers in respect of anything which is in good faith done or intended to be done under this Act.

INDEX